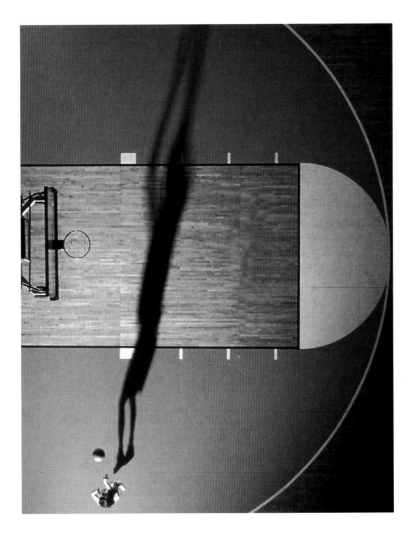

VALUES
OF THE GAME

BILL BRADLEY

ARTISAN ▲ NEW YORK

Published in 1998 by Artisan
A Division of Workman Publishing Company, Inc.
08 Broadway, New York, New York 10003

Library of Congress Cataloging-in-Publication Data

Bradley, Bill, 1943–
     Values of the game/Bill Bradley.
          p.   cm.
      ISBN 1-57965-116-X
        1. Basketball—Moral and ethical aspects. 2. Values.
. National Basketball Association. 4. Bradley, Bill,
943–   . I. Title.
GV888.25.B73 1998
796.323' 0973—dc21   98-7280
                                             CIP

Editor: LAURIE ORSECK
Designer: SUSI OBERHELMAN
Production Director: NANCY MURRAY

Printed in the United States

10 9 8 7 6 5 4 3 2 1

Second Wind © 1979 by Bill Russell. Reprinted by
permission of the author.

CONTENTS

DEDICATION

For my coaches, all of whom loved the game: Jerry Ryan, Arvel Popp (left), Eddie Donovan, Butch Van Breda Kolff (center), Hank Iba, Caesar Rubini, Dick McGuire, Red Holzman (right); and for those who helped along the way—Ed Macauley, Jerry West, Hank Raymonds, Red Auerbach, John McClendon, and Sonny Hill.

FOREWORD

BILL BRADLEY CAME FROM the Air Force to the New York
Knicks in December 1967, my first year in the NBA. He tried to be just another guy, but
everyone wanted a piece of him. It was not hard to see why. There was the big contract ($500,000 for four years) and the oversized expectations of New York fans that he
would lead a Knicks revival. And then there was us, his Knicks teammates, wondering
if this smart guy from Princeton and Oxford was indeed the real deal.

He was, in more ways than I realized at the time. Bill brought with him the
right work ethic—coming to practice early and staying late to work on his game. But
what we didn't anticipate was his ability to adapt his game to whatever the Knicks
needed for the team to succeed. He moved from guard to forward (his position
when we won the championships in 1970 and 1973), and from a great scorer to a role
player. His ego remained undamaged even though he was no longer the star, or "the
man," because he understood the essence of the Knicks team game—that one guy
couldn't carry the load alone.

Bill won us over off the court too. As the team representative to the players'
union which negotiated labor agreements with the league, he brought this same
adaptability, a sense of how to get things accomplished even if he wasn't at the helm,
directing the action or receiving all the credit (Oscar Robertson was the president).

Later in our years in the NBA I became Bill's roommate on the road. I found
myself carried along with his curious nature, his capacity to learn: an art museum in
Houston, a shoreline visit in Oregon, a lecture in Boston. And so I found myself getting another education of sorts. Bill's grasp of our society, what makes it tick and how

business gets done, was really fascinating to watch. One summer he accompanied me to Pine Ridge, South Dakota, to help conduct a basketball camp for the Oglala Sioux. After he arrived, Bill plunged into one of the most closed societies I know, and within twenty-four hours he'd worked out the details of the tribe's power structure. So it wasn't surprising to me that when Bill took the floor of the U.S. Senate he would bring along the same curiosity, the same group sensitivity, and the same determination to get things done that he first took to the floor of Madison Square Garden.

Bill Bradley's value system is not only durable, it's portable. That's the essence of *Values of the Game.* Bill has long had a magnetism that has radiated beyond his own quiet nature. I first saw it thirty years ago at a sports banquet given in my honor in my hometown of Williston, North Dakota. I had asked Bill to be a speaker, and on short notice he rearranged his schedule and made the long trek out to Williston on the Great Plains of North America. As Teddy Roosevelt had done eighty years earlier, he arrived with a knowledgeable enthusiasm, having taken the time to learn about the pioneers, cattle ranchers, and Native Americans. Bill's reputation as a leader and a Christian had prompted the local chapter of the Fellowship of Christian Athletes to seek him out. Bill took on the issue of spirituality with great ease. He spoke to them about the great responsibility to keep a personal set of values. The year was 1968, a time when nearly every institution in society was under question. After the banquet, I drove Bill back to the Plainsman Hotel and we talked over the evening's events, about the FCA and his responsibility to meet other people's expectations. As a PK (preacher's kid), I was familiar with how those responsibilities sometimes conflicted with finding one's own way based on self-knowledge. Bill told me how his personal spiritual commitment had evolved and how being young and wanting to do good sometimes got translated by others into trying to be godly. He said that with his education and upbringing, he was committed to finding some way to serve other people. But, importantly, he also said that being a public person didn't mean that you had to surrender the essence of who you were, that you couldn't let the public impose its expectations on your life, that you had to remain faithful to your own convictions and preserve a private space necessary for personal growth.

Bill was twenty-four and I was twenty-two at the time, and looking back over the last thirty years, I've watched Bill's values hold steady through the changing landscape of our society. Values aren't something that can be donned or discarded, like a used uniform. It seems strange to me that many of the readers of this book will know Bill mostly as a politician, and never had the opportunity to see him play. *Values of the Game* will give you an understanding of why Bill excelled, and why basketball is a perfect arena from which to draw much bigger lessons. Yes, the game has changed a lot since we played: the 3-point line, "small" forwards at 6 feet 8 inches and 250 pounds, and player contracts the size of a small country's economy. But what Bill brought to the game—his industry, his leadership, his pure basketball intelligence—hasn't lost any relevance. And neither have the values, the insights, and the wisdom that he took from the game. He was always generous with the basketball, and I'm delighted that once again he's taken the opportunity to share the wealth.

PHIL JACKSON
1998

INTRODUCTION

O N E   D A Y   I N   1 9 9 6 ,   I was completing my regular physical workout on the StairMaster and treadmill at our local YMCA in Montclair, New Jersey, before returning to work in Washington. After the aerobics, I took a look into the small gym. It was empty—only a runner circling the old-fashioned running track around the ceiling—so I checked out a basketball and went in. It bounced well and the leather felt good. I began to shoot at ten feet, then fifteen, then eighteen. *Swish!* went the ball as it ripped through the net. Within minutes I was in another world, alone with my body movements and my memories. Years had passed since I'd done this, and yet in several minutes I was back. "I love this game!" I thought. The old inner voice began urging me to "hit all the shots." These were different times and such aspiration was foolhardy, but still a surprising number went cleanly through the hoop. After about fifteen minutes, an elderly gentleman poked his head into the gym. I was shooting from the top of the key, then I was driving with a right hook off the boards, followed by a scoop shot. Then I was back at the top of the key. Slowly the man made his way into the gym and out onto the court. He approached me. I pretended to be unaware of him and kept shooting. He leaned in and said, "Bradley?"

"Yes," I said, launching another eighteen-footer.

"Senator Bradley?" he asked.

"Yes," I said.

There was a pause, and then, piercing my idyllic reverie, he blurted out, "Why didn't you answer my letter?"

IN A WORLD FULL of unrealized dreams and baffling entanglements, basketball seems pure. We know, of course, that it isn't. It has its own share of greed,
violence, and obsession with the culture of entertainment. Yet even in the midst of
these distractions, there is still the game. Each time a father takes his son or daughter to the playground to shoot baskets for the first time, a new world opens—one full
of values that can shape a lifetime. In my experience, the feeling of getting better
came with hard work, and getting better made victory easier. Winning was fun, but
so was the struggle to improve. That was one of the lessons you learned from the
game: Basketball was a clear example of virtue rewarded.

I was very lucky to play a game I loved for twenty years, as a high school, college,
and pro player. It gave me a unique window on the world, and it filled me with
moments of insight and years of tremendous pleasure. Some of the most enjoyable

BILL BRADLEY

times in my life were spent playing ball. It is that part of the game that this book celebrates—the good times playing basketball. In the course of writing it, I got to know the coach and players on the team at Stanford University, where I was a visiting professor. Watching them in games and talking about basketball with some of them reawakened memories in me of my life as a player. It was like meeting an old friend after twenty years—someone whose stories I remembered, and whose values I understood and wanted to share. Two decades ago I wrote in *Life on the Run* about my experiences as a New York Knick in the 1960s and 1970s, and there are a few excerpts from that book in this one. But what I try to do here is show how, after all the years, the game is still full of joy and the lessons learned from it stay with you—that even though the game has changed, the old values still flow through it.

I hope parents will share this book with their children and basketball fans will find that it rings true. I believe that it applies to the whole of our passage through life.

PASSION

YOU BEGIN BY BOUNCING a ball—in the house, on the drive-way, along the sidewalk, at the playground. Then you start shooting: legs bent, eyes on the rim, elbow under the ball. You shoot and follow through. Let it fly, up, up and in. No equipment is needed beyond a ball, a rim, and imagination. How simple the basic act is. I'm not sure exactly when my interest turned to passion, but I was very young, and it has never diminished.

When I was a teenager, alone in the high school gym for hours, the repetition of shooting, shot after shot, became a kind of ritual for me. The seams and the grain of the leather ball had to feel a certain way. My fingertips went right to the grooves and told me if it felt right. The key to the fingertips was keeping them clean. I would rub my right hand to my sweaty brow, then against my T-shirt at chest level, and then I would cradle the ball. By the end of shooting practice, the grime had made its way from the floor to the ball to my fingertips to my shirt. After thousands of shots, my shirts were permanently stained.

The gymnasium itself was a part of my solitary joy. I took in every nuance of the place. It was a state-of-the-art facility, with retractable fan-shaped glass back-boards. The floor was polished and shining; when I moved, it glistened as if I were playing on a mirror. The only daylight streamed in from windows high along the sloping ceiling. The smell was not of locker room mildew but of pungent varnish and slightly oiled mops, the guarantors of floor quality throughout the years. The gym's janitor insisted on one

BEGINNINGS

Country roads mean different things to different people. With a little imagination, young dreamers can transform them into Madison Square Garden.

absolute rule: no street shoes allowed on the floor. It was sacred terrain, traversable only by the soft soles of Converse or Keds.

Then there were the sounds. *Thwat, thwat!* The ball hit the floor and the popping sound echoed from the steel beams of the ceiling and the collapsed wooden stands that stacked up twenty feet high. *Thwat, thwat, squeak*—the squeal of your sneakers against the floor, followed by the jump and then the shot. The *swish* of the ball through the net, a sound sweeter than the roar of the crowd. *Swish. Thwat, thwat, squeak, swish!*

I couldn't get enough. If I hit ten in a row, I wanted fifteen. If I hit fifteen, I wanted twenty-five. Driven to excel by some deep, unsurveyed urge, I stayed out on that floor hour after hour, day after day, year after year. I played until my muscles stiffened and my arms ached. I persevered through blisters, contusions, and strained joints. When I got home I had to take a nap before I could muster the energy to eat the dinner that sat in the oven. After one Friday night high school game, which we lost to our arch rival, I was back in the gym at nine on Saturday morning, with the bleachers still deployed and the popcorn boxes scattered beneath them, soaking my defeat by shooting. Others had been in this place last night, I thought, but now I was here by myself, and I was home.

When I practiced alone, I often conjured up the wider world of basketball. Maybe I had just seen the Los Angeles Lakers play on TV the day before; I'd try to remember a particular move that Laker forward Elgin Baylor had made, then imitate it. I would simulate the whole game in my mind, including the spiel of the announcer. "Five seconds left, four seconds, three, Bradley dribbles right in heavy traffic, jumps, shoots—good at the buzzer!" I dreamed that someday I'd experience that moment for real, maybe even take the clutch shot in the state finals. In my dream, of course, I'd hit it and we'd be state champions.

The passion of solitary practice was matched by the joy of playing team ball. The constant kaleidoscope of team play was infinitely interesting to me. For every

ROLE MODEL
Elgin Baylor, 1962

When I practiced alone in high school, I would try
to emulate the moves of the game's great players.
Elgin Baylor's game provided early inspiration.
The Lakers' big-play man was the master of the
rocker step and ingenious around the basket with
either hand. In the 1960–61 season, he averaged
nearly 35 points and 20 rebounds a game.

challenge thrown up by the defense, there was an offensive counter. Having the court

sense to recognize this in the flow of the game produced a real high. The notion that

someday I could be paid to play a game I loved never occurred to me.

YOU COULD ALWAYS TELL that Magic Johnson loved to play.

He smiled, grimaced, and pushed himself and his teammates. His gusto honored the

game. Some players these days seem more angry than joyful, yet the great ones still

have a zest. Grant Hill's pleasure comes from his game's completeness and his own

unflappable composure. Hakeem Olajuwon exudes a delighted confidence when the

ball goes into him at the low post. Clyde Drexler, like Dr. J in earlier years, conveys

an effortless joy when he has the ball in open court and heads for the basket.

Even the controversial Dennis Rodman evinces a love of the game despite

his antics. His game within the game is rebounding. He studies films to see which way

a shooter's shot usually bounces. He keeps his body in top shape. He uses his body

only after he uses his brain and his eyes, and then he makes a second, third, and fourth effort. When he gets the ball, he smiles the smile of someone dedicated to something well beyond himself.

The women's game in particular is full of a kind of beautiful enthusiasm. On many teams each player seems deeply involved in her teammates' spirits as well as their play. I used to love to watch Kate Starbird spark her Stanford team with her tenacity, intensity, and 3-point-shooting skill, but the epitome, for me, is Chamique Holdsclaw of Tennessee, the female Michael Jordan. She has a winning combination of zeal and ability that allows her to generate excitement in the crowd, dedication among her teammates, and fear in the minds of her opponents. Her sheer love of the game becomes infectious.

Imagine what happens when you've got an entire team of players who are passionate about the game. In my Knicks days, there was no feeling comparable to the one I got when the team's game came together—those nights when five guys moved as one. The moment was one of beautiful isolation, the result of the correct blending of human forces at the proper time and to the exact degree. With my team, before the crowd, against our opponents, it was almost as if this were my private world and no one else could sense the inexorable rightness of the moment.

The Knicks 1973 championship was more fun for me than the initial one

A SPECIAL ENTHUSIASM

Women's Final Four

Chamique Holdsclaw of Tennessee (23), aka the female Michael Jordan, shows a similar level of intensity and enthusiasm for the game. That's one reason her team has dominated college hoops. Women have brought a unique spirit to basketball, one I have enjoyed watching. It is marked by a deep commitment to one another and to the team game.

in 1970. We weren't under the pressure of trying to achieve a first championship. The team itself was more congenial; the variety of plays was greater. I had a secure position as a starter. The obstacles that had once blocked my pure enjoyment of the game had all been removed. The only thing I had to do was allow the kid in me to feel the pure pleasure in just playing. In plenty of games, I played simply for the joy of it, shooting and passing without thinking

about points. I forgot the score, and sometimes I would go through a whole quarter

without looking at the scoreboard.

I felt about the court, the ball, the basket, the way people feel about friends, so

playing for money seemed to me to be compromising enough. I never made any

endorsements or commercials during my NBA

career. To take money for hawking basketball

shoes or shaving lotion would have demeaned my

experience of the game, or so I felt. Besides, I

sensed that the deals were being offered because

I was a "white hope" and not because of my play-

ing ability. More than the money, the travel, the

THE SWEETEST VICTORY
New York Knicks, 1973

(Left to right) Jerry Lucas, Walt Frazier, Willis
Reed, Phil Jackson, and me. The blend of
personalities on our second championship
team was so good, and our game so meshed,
that playing basketball became an absolute joy.

lure of the championships, it was the game itself that rewarded me.

I've told the story a thousand times about the night in the 1970s at a postgame reception in Chicago when a man approached me and asked, "Do you really like to play basketball?"

"Yeah, more than anything else I could be doing now," I replied.

"That's great. You know, I once played the trumpet," he said. "I think I know what you feel. I played in a little band. We were good. We'd play on weekends at colleges. In my last year, we had an offer to tour and make records. Everyone wanted to except me."

"Why didn't you?"

"My father thought it wasn't secure enough."

"What about you?"

"Well, I didn't know," he said. "I guess I agreed. The life is so transient. You're always on the road. No sureness that you'll get your next job. It just doesn't fit into a life plan. So I went to law school and I quit playing the trumpet, except every once in a while. Now I don't have time."

"Do you like the law?"

"It's okay. But it's nothing like playing the trumpet."

THE COMPETITIVE WILL

Dennis Rodman, Grant Hill, Clyde Drexler

Chicago Bulls forward Dennis Rodman (opposite page) isn't everyone's cup of tea, but I admire the determination he shows on the floor. He's turned rebounding into an art form. Grant Hill (left), on the other hand, is a complete player, whose nice-guy personality can't camouflage his fierce desire to win. It's the same combination of grace and grit that has marked the admirable career of Houston's Clyde "the Glide" Drexler (right). Watching Clyde's effortless movement, you can almost lose sight of the work that goes into it.

I LOVE THIS GAME

Michael Jordan, Magic Johnson, Stephon Marbury

In my rookie year, the average NBA salary was $9,500. Today's pros make 150 times that and more, but if basketball itself can't get a player excited, money certainly won't. You can see the emotion on the face of Michael Jordan (left) when he exhorts his teammates, and in Magic Johnson's exultation over a perfect play (right). A new crop of young stars, like Minnesota's Stephon Marbury (opposite page), brings the same kind of enthusiasm to their jobs.

DISCIPLINE

IN CRYSTAL CITY, MISSOURI, when I was growing up, my basketball heroes were Bob Pettit, Elgin Baylor, Oscar Robertson, Wilt Chamberlain, and Jerry West. When I was fourteen, I went to a week-long basketball camp run by Easy Ed Macauley, a forward for the St. Louis Hawks who had returned to his hometown in a trade (an epochal one, it turns out) that sent Bill Russell to the Boston Celtics. Macauley and his staff gave morning lectures on proper attitude and other aspects of basketball, and at one of these lectures he said, "If you're not practicing, just remember—someone, somewhere, is practicing, and when you two meet, given roughly equal ability, he will win." Those words made a deep impression on me. I decided I never wanted to lose simply because I hadn't made the effort, and I intensified an already intense routine.

Beginning that year and all through high school, I practiced from June to September, four days a week, three hours a day; from September to March, I practiced three to four hours a day Monday through Friday and five hours a day on Saturday and Sunday. In the fall, before basketball season began, I ran along streets in town, through fields, over railroad tracks, down to the banks of the Mississippi and back. To improve my vertical leap, I wore weights in my shoes and jumped to touch the rim for four sets of fifteen jumps each, with alternating hands. I practiced dribbling by wearing plastic glasses that prevented me from looking

THE BIG O
Bucks vs. Lakers, 1973

Oscar Robertson was in many respects the perfect player, solid in all the game's fundamentals. He could pass, dribble, defend, and rebound, and he never took a twenty-foot shot if he could get one closer to the basket. With his textbook fall-away jump shot, he averaged nearly 26 points a game over his fourteen-year career.

Barnett was a player who emphatically demon-
strated the virtues of discipline. He played
basketball every day of his last three years of
high school: 1,095 straight days. Sometimes
he played from nine in the morning until
midnight. He practiced in the heat of summer
and in the dead of night. He played basketball
while his friends went to the senior prom.
But he got to dance in the NBA.

down at the ball and forced me to keep my eyes on the court ahead of me. I formed

an obstacle course with the gym's metal folding chairs, weaving among them with

a crossover dribble. I stacked chairs in towers to practice shooting hook shots over

an imaginary seven-footer. Alone in the gym, I made moves to the baseline, reverse-

pivoted back toward the lane, gave a head fake, then changed the ball from one hand

to the other for the layup. I shot set shots and then jump shots from five different

places on the floor, with the backspin often bringing the ball back to me as if it were

a yo-yo on a string. I kept shooting until I had hit twenty-five in a row from each

spot with the set shot and twenty-five in a row with the jump shot. If I missed num-

ber twenty-three, I started over. And above all, I played wherever there was a good

game, sometimes driving twice a day to St. Louis during the summer for pickup

scrimmages. When a fifteen-year-old female classmate telephoned one night to flirt,

I somewhat doltishly protested that my real girlfriend was basketball.

In retrospect, I think I probably spent an excessive amount of time in the gym

during those years, but the by-product of those countless hours of practice was a self-discipline that carried over into every aspect of my life. My freshman year at Princeton was a struggle academically. Many of my classmates were from prep schools and had essentially covered the first year's classwork the year before; I was from a small-town high school in the Midwest and Ivy League standards were new to me and very, very difficult. Spring midterms went badly, so I quit freshman baseball—my second sport—and virtually lived in the library. I barely made it through that first year, but by my senior year, having kept up the work pattern I established out of necessity as a freshman, I achieved a respectable record.

In the U.S. Senate, along the campaign trail, or on any number of projects I became involved with after Princeton, it was the same story. I was determined that no one would outwork me. Basketball had lit that fire, and it burned in many directions. As I grew older and met my basketball heroes, and even defeated some of them, I realized that my way of doing things was not at all unique. Most of the pros had developed their skills by paying their dues in practice time. The biggest myth in basketball is that of the "natural player." Remember that Michael Jordan was cut from his high school team.

THE NEED FOR DISCIPLINE applies first to conditioning. It's painful and grueling, but there's no alternative. You can't lead the fast break or tear down 20 rebounds a game if you can't run and jump without fatigue. Getting into shape and pushing the body to new levels every day is a mental activity. When you believe that you can't do another lap or another push-up or another abdominal crunch, your mind forces you to go ahead. When your wind is short and you have a pain in your side from running, only your mind can get you to withstand the pain and go on. As UCLA's legendary coach John Wooden says, "Nothing will work unless you do."

I used to hate getting into shape no matter which routines I followed—laps, line drills, playing one on one full court, running the floor while passing the ball back and forth with two teammates. After six weeks of agony, during which every

At Oxford (far right), I found out that if I ran regularly I could play effectively twice a month for an Italian team in European Cup competition, but to get through an eighty-two-game pro season requires a higher level of conditioning. When my teammate Phil Jackson (right, with Knicks trainer Danny Whelan) had a spinal fusion, he quickly realized that physical therapy required dedication too. The last part of discipline is constant skill development. It starts when you are young and continues until your playing days end—in the words of John Wooden (center), "Failing to prepare is preparing to fail" and "It is what you learn after you know it all that counts."

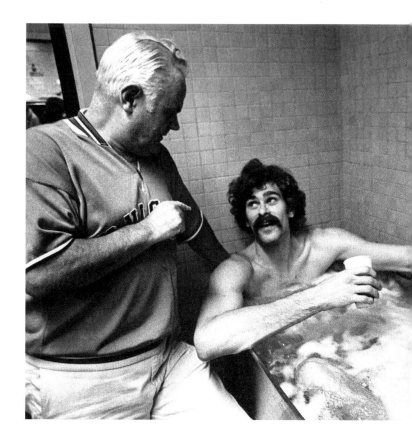

part of my body ached so badly that many mornings I crawled from bed to bathroom to soak in a hot tub, the pain began to diminish and the muscles started to come around. When you train seriously for basketball, you learn the difference between getting into condition and *getting into condition*. In the lesser of those two states, you can run up and down the floor and do what you have to do without the interference of fatigue. But you're not really in peak condition until you can cruise when others push. When your body is honed, you can run your opponents around and around, with little immediate purpose beyond tiring them out, making them angry, or distracting them from any defensive concentration. My toughest opponent, John Havlicek of the Boston Celtics, was a true genius when it came to using conditioning as a weapon. His goal was to get his opponent to give up, to stop overcoming fatigue, to stop pushing himself. Havlicek saw it as a matter of who gives up first. "You'll pass out before you're overworked, but most people don't know that," he once told

Orlando Magic senior executive vice president Pat Williams. "They think they're over-worked, so they stop. They could have kept going, but they didn't. They weren't beat physically; they were beat mentally."

Skill development comes next. The critical years are in high school, and the real preparation begins when the season ends. Off-season is when major leaps occur in a high school player's abilities, when you develop the crossover dribble, the reverse pivot, and opposite-hand shooting.

The only way to become a shooter is by shooting—not only in scrimmages but alone. It's like learning to walk: Once babies master the basics, they no longer have to think about "how" to walk. The same is true of shooting. Once you've mastered your techniques and found your rhythm, you never lose them. They become your individual basketball signature. As you grow older, your legs can go bad and running will become more difficult, but you never lose the shooting. It may be harder to get into position to take the shots, but to hit them shouldn't be a struggle. Then again, if you don't have the will to get the shot down—to do it over and over—you'll never be a shooter at all.

The great thing about discipline is that you can get immediate returns on your investment of time and effort: The harder you work, the sooner your skills improve. Then the virtuous circle takes over. As your skills grow, you get a rush of self-confidence, which spurs you to continue working, and your skills increase all the faster. Practice pays off more when you concentrate while you're doing it. But that's harder than it sounds. In shooting practice, there's no crowd; sometimes it's just you, the ball, and the basket. In order to hit twenty-five in a row in high school, I had to concentrate, think about what I was doing, and get the feel for all the elements involved—the legs, the elbow, the follow-through. My mind was focused on each attempt. I was grooving my shot.

By the time I was twenty-one, total involvement in shooting practice was more difficult. I had to reduce the number of consecutive shots to fifteen in a row, and by the time I was thirty-three, I couldn't force myself to do more than ten out of thirteen. While it was true that after twenty years of practice I knew what I was doing technically, I also found my mind wandering in the midst of the routine—to the day's headlines, to a comment a friend had made, to anything but shooting. As a result, I couldn't hit practice shots as consistently as I had in high school and college. That realization was part of what told me it was time to quit.

AS DIFFICULT AS individual discipline is, it pales next to team demands. Hitting the open man with the pass and staying with a

LARRY BIRD, ASSASSIN
Boston Celtics

One of the great stories about Bird is how he walked into the locker room before the first NBA All-Star 3-point shooting contest and announced, "Which one of you guys is shooting for second place?" He won it, of course. That kind of confidence comes from constant practice and total concentration on what you're doing. Bird was always focused on the task at hand. Michael Cooper used to say, in reference to Bird's intensity, that looking into his eyes during the last three minutes of a close game was like looking into the eyes of an assassin.

pattern or play until its conclusion require uncommon self-control. It takes real character to derive enjoyment from the pass that leads to the pass that leads to the basket. If one player fails to make the interim pass, to block out for a rebound, or to take the open shot, it affects the whole team. Coach Jerry Sloan's Utah Jazz and Pat Summitt's Tennessee Lady Vols epitomize seamless team offense.

A man-to-man defense requires team discipline too. There's no such thing as "I stopped my man" if three other opposing players scored at will. When a player goes for a steal and misses, his teammates have to pick up his man quickly. When a player covers for the teammate making the steal attempt, another teammate has to move over and cover for the one helping the stealer. A willingness to make yourself vulnerable to catcalls from the fans if your man scores while you are helping your teammates is the ultimate test of a disciplined team defense.

Determination sits at the core of discipline, and the will to excel sits at the core of determination. You don't have to be a pro to learn that lesson from basketball. When I failed as a rookie guard in the NBA, my desire to succeed placed a resolute grid of practice over my entire off-season. I had known in high school and college how it felt to be regarded as the best. I preferred that feeling to the sense of failure I had after my first pro year. Only later did I realize that I had worked all summer not just to hone my skills but to regain my self-respect.

In 1973, the Knicks played the Celtics for the NBA Eastern Conference Championship. We lost the sixth game, in New York, sending the final game back to Boston, where the Celtics had never lost the seventh game of a playoff—ever. The day before the game, Ned Irish, the president

BREAKING TOGETHER
Houston Rockets, 1994

Self-discipline has a demanding twin: team discipline. You can't execute a full-court press if only half the team is pressing. In many ways, team discipline is harder, because it requires individual acts of unselfishness—setting screens, boxing out for rebounds, taking only good shots—that don't show up in the stats. Throwing the pass that leads to the pass that leads to a basket, as Sam Cassell is doing here for the championship Rockets, is what gets easy points. And points show up on the scoreboard.

of the Knicks, made one of his very rare appearances at practice. He said, partly in anger and partly out of calculation, that we should be ashamed of ourselves, that we had had a great year within our grasp but had thrown it all away the night before. He ended by saying that we didn't have much of a chance in Boston. Some teams would have quit on themselves at this point, but Irish's scathing commentary fired us up. The next day we played one of our best-disciplined defensive games, and we won not only the game but the NBA championship that year as well.

Learning the discipline it takes to succeed in basketball teaches a fine appreciation for how hard you have to work. The difficulty of preparation contributes to the sense of triumph. As Lao-tzu put it, "Mastery of others is strength; mastery of yourself is true power." When you overcome adversity with self-discipline and you win a hard-fought battle, the elation explodes. There are few things in life better than that.

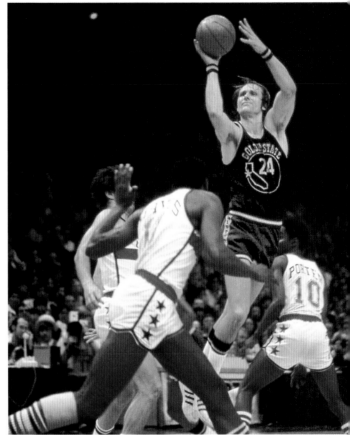

SHOOTING STARS

Glen Rice, Rick Barry, Jerry West

They're called pure shooters—players who seem to be able to get up out of bed in the morning and hit 25 in a row. Such natural ability is a sculptured technique formed by shooting over and over and over again until your arms ache. Among today's players, Charlotte's Glen Rice (left) on a hot streak is something to see: Rising like a pogo stick, eyes locked on the rim, he is always near the top of the league in 3-point shooting percentage. Golden State's Rick Barry (right) had a deadly jump shot and a fierce competitiveness. He was lethal from the foul line too, with a .900 career average. And then there was Jerry West (opposite page). If you want to teach someone how to shoot, just look at the films of West—the momentum-stopping foot jammed into the floor, the last hard dribble before the jump, and the shot with its perfect release.

BILL BRADLEY

DETERMINATION

Dave DeBusschere, Muggsy Bogues, Michael Jordan

"How much do you want it?" It's a question that coaches ask repeatedly. Determination holds the key to success at many levels. His considerable ability aside, has there ever been anyone so unwilling to lose as Michael Jordan (right)? Just think of his steal and winning basket in the last game of the 1998 NBA finals. Determination comes in a variety of forms. For the solid pros of the early seventies, like Dave DeBusschere (opposite page), a mere broken nose could not be painful enough to suppress his desire to play—and to win. And in a league of giants, why is it that guys as small as the 5 feet 3 Muggsy Bogues (left) can overcome that striking disadvantage? It's desire, backed by determination and a work ethic, that few people of any size can match.

SELFLESSNESS

PART OF THE BEAUTY and mystery of basketball rests in the variety of its team requirements. Championships are not won unless a team has forged a high degree of unity, attainable only through the selflessness of each of its players. It is in the moves that the uninitiated often don't see that the sport has its deepest currents: the perfect screen, the purposeful movement away from the ball, the well-executed boxout, the deflected pass. Statistics don't always measure teamwork; holding the person you're guarding scoreless doesn't show up in your stats. But when you're "taking care of business," you're working to produce a championship team, and "We won" comes to mean more and lasts longer than the ephemeral "I scored." Solidarity becomes an essential part of your professionalism.

The society we live in glorifies individualism, what Ross Perot used to champion with the expression "eagles don't flock." Basketball teaches a different lesson: that untrammeled individualism destroys the chance for achieving victory. Players must have sufficient self-knowledge to take the long view—to see that what any one player can do alone will never equal what a team can do together.

SCREEN-AND-ROLL
John Stockton and Karl Malone

If you've watched the Utah Jazz play in the last ten years, you've seen the screen-and-roll in its ultimate execution. Just try getting around a screen set by Karl Malone—especially when he's stepping on your foot.

All players, even the greatest, sometimes get out of sync with the rhythm and purpose of the team. By the time Michael Jordan came back to basketball from his year of baseball, the Chicago Bulls had hired nine new players. Michael didn't have time to synchronize his game with theirs. In the 1995 playoffs, he tried do it all himself, and the new guys were content to watch

"The Michael Show." The result was convincing proof that one man can't beat five. Usually, the problem on a team is not the one great player trying to shoulder the entire load but the average-to-good player trying to get attention. You see it in high school games, even in college. Most kids want to shoot; not many want to pass. Too few see selflessness as a goal.

Defense is where team basketball begins. When Red Holzman took over as coach of the New York Knicks in the winter of 1967, he made the point clearly by calling twenty-three practices in twenty-three days, and two thirds of that time was taken up by defense. This was his way of bringing some unity to a group of very disparate individuals. "See the ball!" he would shout—in other words, don't be so absorbed in guarding your own man that you don't see when a teammate needs assistance guarding his. Phil Jackson had similar concerns when he took over as coach of the Bulls in 1989. By getting his players to keep the ball in sight at the same time they overplayed their men, he was able to move help from the weak side whenever it was needed. Slowly he got them to realize how much better they were as a group when they helped each other. By emphasizing defense as the core strength of the team, he was able to show the other players that Michael Jordan was only one fifth of the effort (even if Jordan's fifth was spectacular).

There is nothing as exciting in basketball as a team that knows how to apply defensive pressure, either through a full-court press or a trapping half-court press. That's when offense flows out of defense, when a few steals, turnovers, or intercepted passes can change the whole momentum of a game. The University of Kentucky won the NCAA tournament in 1998 in part because it was a team that knew how to press. During the 1970 championship season, in a regular season game against the

RED HOLZMAN
New York Knicks, 1970

By definition, everyone in the NBA is a star, the best in the world. The question is how to get such individual talents to play together. As coach of the Knicks, Red Holzman emphasized that the team that defends together—and in the NBA, team defense is essential—will control the tempo of the game. By taking the will out of the opponent, team defense leads to team offense. Then the game becomes something more than a series of one-on-one contests.

BOB COUSY ON THE BREAK
Boston Celtics, 1962

One of the more frequent sights during the Celtics dynasty was Bob Cousy leading his team down the floor. Cousy's court sense was unparalleled in his day. He knew long before his opponents did where the pass was going, and it arrived almost every time with a softness and precision that allowed a teammate to catch it and score easily.

Cincinnati Royals, the Knicks were behind 5 points with seventeen seconds to go in the fourth quarter. Willis Reed hit two foul shots. Suddenly DeBusschere intercepted an inbounds pass and dunked the ball for 2 points. Then Frazier recovered a loose ball, was fouled, and hit two foul shots for our eighteenth win in a row.

On offense, there are three unselfish team actions that make all the difference. The first is passing. Bob Cousy, the great guard on the Boston Celtics in the fifties and sixties, filled the center lane on a fast break with such textbook simplicity that you wanted to replay it over and over so kids could learn their fundamentals. Cousy took the ball to the middle of the court with two of his teammates filling the lanes on his right and left and a third teammate trailing to pick up the easy eighteen-footer if a layup by one teammate or a short jumper by Cousy didn't develop. He created too many choices for the defense to handle, and the key was his ability to pass the ball. Watching the Los Angeles Lakers from 1982 to 1989 with Magic Johnson running the fast break was a comparable lesson. The ball whizzed down the court with a minimum of dribbling—from Kareem Abdul-Jabbar to Michael Cooper to Magic for the play in the middle, in which he often dished the ball off to James Worthy for a layup. Magic had the ability to see not only when someone was open for a pass, but also what his teammate would do with the ball when he got it. I call that seeing the whole court, a remarkable sixth-sense quality also possessed by the great Pelé in soccer and Wayne Gretzky in hockey.

On an unselfish team, the passer knows the ball will come back. The better passer a center is, the easier it will be for him to score. When opponents double down on him, he can whip the ball to someone who has an open shot. Then when the defense recovers, a teammate whips it right back to the center. Do that a few times and the defense is reeling. But it starts with an unselfish center. That's what Pete Carril, Princeton's former coach of twenty-nine years, would characterize as "help someone else, help yourself."

During a game, what I loved most was spotting an imbalance in the opponent's defense and getting the ball to the open man at the right time, in the right place, with the right zip. I loved sensing where a teammate was and following my intuition with a pass. I would notice when an opponent turned his head the wrong way, then throw the ball past his ears or behind his legs to a cutting teammate. Often, if you had a willing partner, the two of you could get a two-person game going without interfering with the flow of the team. Walt Frazier and I used to run a simple backdoor play. I was the passer. The center would clear to my side of the floor and Frazier would drift toward the top of the key. As I dribbled away from the center and toward Frazier, we would catch each other's eye, and after a hesitation step or a fake in my direction, he would cut quickly behind his man into the open area just in front of the foul line. I would give him a bounce pass. He'd catch it and in one motion go

SHOWTIME
Los Angeles Lakers, 1991

Did anyone love to pass as much as Magic Johnson (32) on a fast break (overleaf)? No wonder teammates like James Worthy (42) and Byron Scott (4) hustled to get out and run with him. They knew that if they got into scoring position, Magic would see them, even if he was looking the other way, and the ball would soon follow.

for the layup and the Garden crowd would explode. The value of such a move was that it got our team 2 points. (It also improved my relationship with Frazier. Who wouldn't appreciate someone who got you an easy 2?) And it tended to demoralize the other team by making them look foolish.

Screening—placing your body in the way of an opponent—is another way to help a teammate get an easier shot. Today the screen-and-roll is a staple of the pro game, and there are no two people better at it than John Stockton and Karl Malone of the Utah Jazz. Malone sets a screen on Stockton's defender. If Malone's defender fails to switch out on Stockton, then Stockton has a clear jump shot. If Malone's man does switch out on Stockton, Malone rolls away so that Stockton's man is behind him, creating a passing lane in the space vacated by the defender who switched out. Stockton bounces a quick pass to Malone, who has an easy layup. For these two players, this series of maneuvers becomes an offensive weapon. More times than not, one of them scores on it.

Setting a screen away from the ball is an unexpected move that often springs a teammate into the open to receive a pass. If there is a double team on the man coming off the screen, the screener simply cuts to the basket unguarded. If a passer is alert and gets the ball to the former screener, the latter gets an easy layup. The beauty of screening is that on a team of good passers each screen has several options. The defense can never be sure what will happen next. It is an impossible situation to cover without a perfectly executed team defense, and develops only because one player helps another.

Moving without the ball is the third unselfish act of a great offense, one that too few players know how to do. They either stand around and watch their teammates go one on one or they run after the ball, clogging up large areas of the court in the process. A forward simply clearing out of one side so that there is only a guard and a center left is the most elementary

HONDO
John Havlicek, Boston Celtics

This guy drove me crazy. He drove everybody crazy. Covering John Havlicek was like trying to hold mercury in your hand. He worked harder than any player out there, constantly running, using screens, getting the ball at the right time, taking only the good shots. The ultimate competitor.

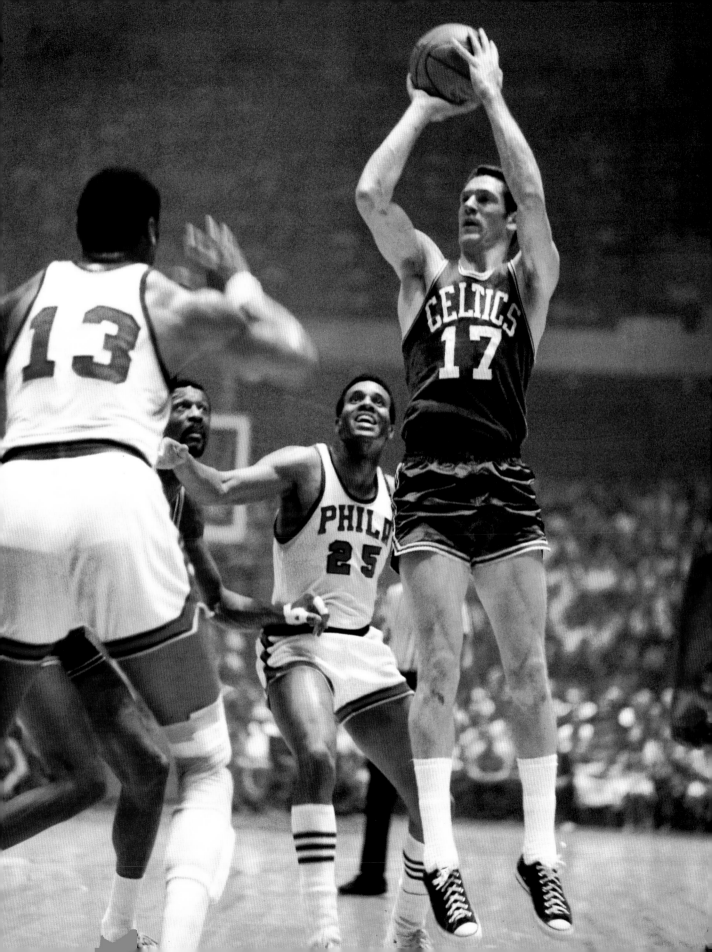

example of this strategy. When timed to the movement of the ball, creating space makes things happen. Nobody I know ever said to a teammate, "Why don't you bring the guy guarding you into where I'm working, because I like trying to pass or score a basket in traffic." When you move without the ball on an unselfish team, and you work hard to lose your man, you know that if you pop open you'll get the ball. John Havlicek was difficult to guard because he never stopped moving, and every time he got a half step on me (which was more often than I care to be specific about), he got the ball and got it in good scoring position.

I can learn more about people by playing a three-on-three game with them for twenty minutes than I can by talking with them for a week. I once hired a new director for my U.S. Senate offices in New Jersey. I liked him, but it wasn't until I played basketball with him that I knew I'd made the right choice. I found out that he was a hard worker (he went for the rebound), competitive with a fierce desire to win (he played close defense), and unselfish (he screened away from the ball).

There is a special bond on an unselfish team. It remains steadfast even with the passage of time. Whenever I see Willis Reed, I remember how he risked permanent injury in order to play in the seventh game of the 1970 championships. When I see Frazier, or DeBusschere, or Monroe, or Jackson, or Barnett, or Lucas, I remember—how could I not?—all the practices, the flights, the bus trips, the locker room banter out of which came our collective identity. How can I ever forget their professionalism, their desire to win, their willingness to trust me and the other teammates with their greatest dream: to be a champion?

In the winter of 1997, I went to New York for a weekend celebration commemorating the fiftieth anniversary of the Celtics-Knicks rivalry. Players from both teams, from every era, congregated at Madison Square Garden. The best-represented team was also the best basketball team of all time: the 1964–65 Celtics, with Bill Russell, Tom Heinsohn, and Sam Jones, among others. You could tell that these

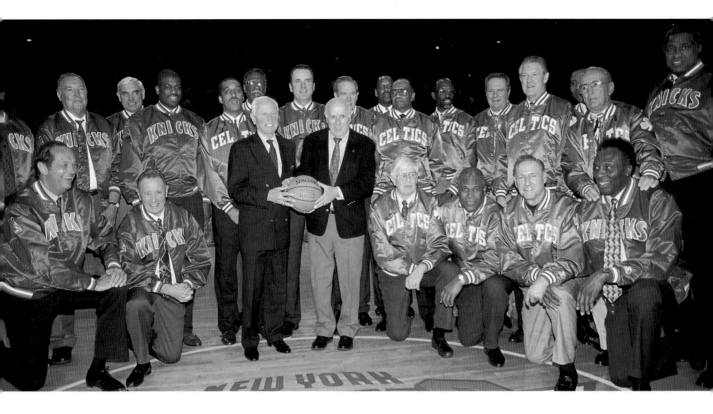

men still existed as a unit. They were grayer and heavier, but they were still warriors in each other's eyes. The pride they felt for what they had accomplished was palpable, and something else that was clear to everyone was the respect and friendship they still felt for one another.

THOSE CHAMPIONSHIP SEASONS

It doesn't surprise me that members of championship teams keep in touch long after the glory has been reduced to grainy film clips. We shared too much to let the memories fade. These are the Celtics of the mid-sixties, with most of another total unit, the Knicks of the early seventies—my Knicks—together in 1997 in New York City.

Championship teams share a moment that few other people know. The overwhelming emotion derives from more than pride. Your devotion to your teammates, the depth of your sense of belonging, is something like blood kinship, but without its complications. Rarely can words fully express it. In the nonverbal world of basketball, it's like grace or beauty or ease in other areas of your life. It is the bond that selflessness forges.

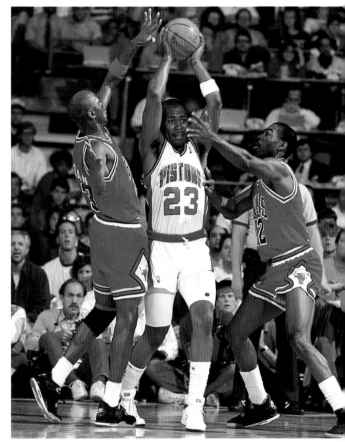

DEFENSIVE PRESSURE

Swarming, unrelenting, suffocating defense—it was the hallmark of Red Holzman's Knicks, and it didn't hurt to have the consummate ball thief in Walt Frazier (opposite page). Not coincidentally, defensive pressure has become one of the hallmarks of the Chicago Bulls (right), who are coached by one of Red's former players, Phil Jackson. Great defense demands complete unselfishness; guarding your own man isn't enough; you have to help out your teammates. That's Alonzo Mourning (left) in a Princeton sandwich during the NCAA tournament of 1989.

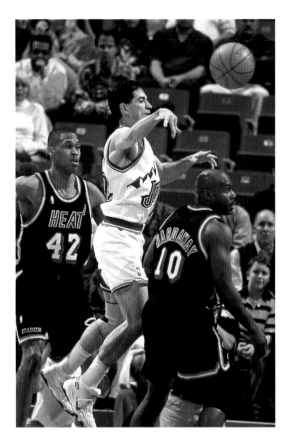
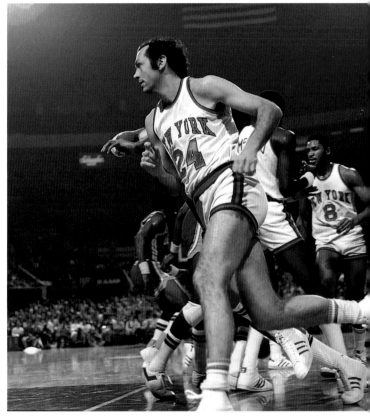

HELP SOMEONE ELSE

John Stockton, Bill Bradley, Bill Walton

John Stockton (left) helps lots of folks—one reason he's led the league in assists for nine consecutive years. And who can forget the picture of big Bill Walton (opposite page) in the low post for the Portland Trail Blazers? His teammates knew that a pass into the post was not a one-way trip. It would inevitably come back to the passer if he got into good position for a shot or made a strong cut toward the basket. And that made Walton more of a scoring threat too, because the defense couldn't sag on him. Moving without the ball (right)—to set a screen away from the ball, to move purposefully for a pass, to distract an opponent from defensive concentration, to clear space for a teammate—is the kind of unselfish action that works only when players play as a team.

BILL BRADLEY

GIVING AND GETTING

RESPECT

PROFESSIONAL ATHLETES begin their experience with sports
much as millions of other kids do. For me, basketball suddenly became a serious
matter in the seventh grade. I was serving as the den chief in a Cub Scout pack that
met on Tuesdays, at the same time as basketball practice. In the middle of the meeting during the first week of practice, I got a call from my mother, informing me that
the coach had just phoned to say that if I was not at practice in twenty-five minutes,
I was off the team. So much for the Cub Scouts. The coach demanded respect for the
sport, and I gave it fully, from that day on.

Today recruiting begins in the seventh grade. Ambitious parents eyeing a pro
career for their kids bargain with the high school coach for a preferred style of play
before they allow their son or daughter to attend the coach's school. Universities
award scholarships to talented players who perfunctorily fill out an admissions
application and who often, unsurprisingly, fail to
graduate. Players turn pro out of high school or
early in college, giving up their chance for an education for the uncertainties of life on the road. Pro
teams cope with players who regularly have brushes
with the law. In one sense, the game is struggling to
keep its integrity alive.

Yet for every unscrupulous recruiter or bad
coach who exploits the young people he is sup-
posed to lead, there are still thousands committed

CHAMBERLAIN AND RUSSELL
The Matchup of the Sixties

Wilt Chamberlain was a dominant scorer and
rebounder for the Warriors, 76ers, and Lakers,
winning two championships. Bill Russell, the
hub of the Boston Celtics dynasty that won
eleven titles, had a shrewd defensive prowess.
Fans are forever debating who was better (I'd
pick Russell). But the respect these two players
had for each other is what brought out their
best games when they competed head to head.

to the deeper values of the game. They quietly go about their job of shaping young lives. They resist the pressures to ratify the behavior that too many TV images glorify and they continue to preach the gospel of "no shortcuts to work," "no championship without individual sacrifice," "no feeling like the satisfaction of a job well done." They know that the noble spirit of athletic competition and achievement can reflect the highest values of our collective life.

Every athlete ultimately has a choice about whether to do the right thing when temptations pull the other way. These moments begin in high school, when a teacher may want to give you a break simply because you play ball. They continue in college, as alumni hover protectively and flatter frequently. As a professional basketball player, you're exposed to drugs, alcohol, and fast-buck artists in every town you visit. You either say no to the allure of the fast lane or you fail to respect yourself enough to keep to what you know is in your own interest in the long run.

By the time players reach college, the chance for coaches to shape character declines, but they can still be instrumental in influencing long-term goals. John Thompson at Georgetown, Dean Smith at the University of North Carolina, Bobby Knight at Indiana, and Mike Krzyzewski are examples of tough taskmasters who oversee the nonathletic commitments of their students: Approximately 90 percent of the players in those four programs graduate. Pete Carril of Princeton tells a story from his childhood that every college athlete should ponder. Carril's father worked in a open-hearth steel mill in Bethlehem, Pennsylvania. Every morning before he left for work and Pete and his sister for school, he'd turn to them at the breakfast table and say, "In this life, the big strong guys are always taking from the smaller, weaker guys but . . . the smart take from the strong."

The really great coaches engage their players in a quest to be the best. Some bark their orders;

DEAN SMITH
North Carolina

Easily one of the most esteemed college coaches, Dean Smith fully understood the term *student athlete*. His coaching style linked a player's responsibilities to his maturity. And his players learned the fundamentals: respect for the game and respect for each other.

others are more like machines, with a clipboard full of practice drills. In the right player-coach relationship, a quiet "well done" can go a long way. (As Mark Twain said, "Most of us can run pretty well all day long on one compliment.") By talking candidly about the problems of adolescence or the vagaries of the parent-child relationship, some high school coaches extend their reach to life off the court. Their players may never become pros, but because they learned the values of the game they are better prepared for life. Many people in all walks of life will tell you that their lives were turned around by a coach who took an interest in their total well-being.

By the time they turn professional, basketball players have generally learned that their entire career is governed by many sets of rules. If you want to play, you have to abide by them. UCLA coach John Wooden made it a team rule that none of

John Wooden, "the Wizard of Westwood," guided all his teams with a set of life values as strong as steel. His players—even Bill Walton, his free-spirited center—came to respect him as the boss. In the process, they learned lessons that last a lifetime, such as "Discipline yourself and others won't need to."

his players sport facial hair. Bill Walton, one of UCLA's star players in the 1970s, once returned from a ten-day layoff with a beard. When he came onto the floor for practice, Wooden asked him whether he'd forgotten something. Walton replied, "Coach, if you mean the beard, I think I should be allowed to wear it. It's my right."

"Do you believe that strongly?" Wooden asked.

"Yes, I do, Coach. Very much," Walton answered.

Wooden's response was polite. "Bill, I have a great respect for individuals who stand up for those things in which they believe. I really do. And the team is going to miss you."

Walton immediately went to the locker room and shaved off his beard. As

Wooden recalls in his memoir, *A Lifetime of Observations and Reflections On and Off the Court,* "There were no hard feelings. . . . He understood that the choice was between his own desires and the good of the team, and Bill was a team player. I think if I had given in to him, I would have lost control, not only of Bill but of his teammates."

My coach at Princeton was Bill (Butch) Van Breda Kolff, who taught basketball with something of the extemporaneous quality of a jazz performance. We didn't have very many set plays. There were no drills for passing or boxing out on rebounds. He taught us about the fundamentals in the context of play, stopping a half-court or full-court game from time to time to tell us what we could have done better. Under his freelance offense, players developed the ability to create, to see things emerging. Above all, the game was fun. My coach for the 1964 Olympics, Hank Iba of Oklahoma State, took the opposite approach. Every morning during practice, he lectured the team, using a blackboard to display diagrams for the offense. We had to keep notebooks of these lectures. During a game, he tolerated no deviation from his plays or their options. Both coaches emphasized conditioning. Their personalities and their styles of coaching were as different as their preferred offenses, but both men engendered respect—Van Breda Kolff because of his intensity in competition, Iba because of his thoroughness in practice.

WHEN YOU'RE PLAYING DEFENSE, you generally get to know your opponent very well. You know whether he prefers going right or left on a drive, or whether he shoots less well from a certain place on the court, but you also form an impression of his personality—how hard he works, how much he wants to win, how he makes up for his weaknesses, how likely he is to blame someone else for his own failure. When both of you hold nothing back and push as hard as possible to win, you are both at your most vulnerable—because one of you will fail. Your opponent sees this in you, as you see it in him. From this rugged intimacy emerges a unique respect. Beating a weaker player by a lot holds only a fraction of the joy that you get from beating an evenly matched player by the slimmest of margins. For me, having a good game against Bob Love of Chicago or Jack Marin of Baltimore or Bill Bridges of Los Angeles or Lou Hudson of Atlanta was more rewarding than running rings around a rookie. Against Boston, I considered the night a great success if I scored 15 while Havlicek scored 25 and the Knicks won.

When Wilt Chamberlain played against Bill Russell, it was a classic matchup rooted in mutual respect. Chamberlain was the dominant individual in a team game. He amassed incredible statistics—50 points per game was his average in one year, 27.2 rebounds per game another year, and his record for a single game was 100 points. Russell, on the other hand, was the ultimate team player—his Celtics won eleven championships in thirteen years. With lightning reflexes and an intense mental concentration, his only objective was the team's victory. Russell would not always outplay Chamberlain, but he would often outfox him. They would encounter each other around half a dozen times a year before the playoffs, and they usually played their best games against each other. Each pushed the other to higher levels of performance.

You don't have to be a star to win respect. The tenth, eleventh, and twelfth men know they'll see little playing time, yet the quality of a team is often enhanced by those at the end of the bench. If they see their jobs as working hard in practice to push the starting five and playing a positive role in the team dynamic off the court, they can be essential to a championship. Swen Nater pushed Bill Walton in every practice at UCLA. He played in few college games, but he was good enough to be drafted by the NBA in the first round. Ken Shank pushed me every day in practice at Princeton, and toward the end of my career as a Knick, Phil Jackson did the same thing. Mike Riordan, Bill Hoskett, Don May,

THE CELTICS DYNASTY
1957–69

It wasn't just basketball, it was Celtics basketball, a term that gave a whole new dimension to the sport. With an ever-changing cast of solid role players around the core of stars such as Bill Russell, Bob Cousy, Sam Jones, and John Havlicek, the Celtics collected titles as they ran opponents ragged. Theirs was a game that emphasized constant motion and ball movement, and total team commitment. "We won because of comradeship, friendship, and teamwork," Bill Russell said after his final championship.

and John Warren got little public credit for our 1970 championship, and Dean Meminger, Hawthorne Wingo, Henry Bibby, and John Gianelli missed out on personal glory in 1973, but in both the Knicks' championship years they got plenty of credit from their teammates.

THERE IS AN EXTRA DIMENSION to the respect that exists among teammates—a respect beyond that accorded the rules, the coach, and the opponent. Teammates on a team that wins will never be strangers. Teammates on a team that wins the state tournament in high school, or the conference championship in college, will forever be bound by their mutual achievement. In the pros, from exhibitions to playoffs, a team plays more than a hundred games a season.

BILL BRADLEY

Players often have four games in five nights in four different cities. By late February, fatigue is the common enemy. Often there's not enough time for sufficient rest even if a player manages his day wisely—yet each night he has to go out and push hard to win. Dave DeBusschere, his face drawn from the long season, and Willis Reed, with his brow furrowed and heating packs on each knee, used to look over at each other in the locker room of the fourth town in five days, and their glances alone seemed to say, "I'm tired to my bones—I don't want to go out there. But if you do it, I will too."

Out of this kind of team commitment comes a deep respect. After a game, each man knows that everyone has given his all. It's an honest and open relationship; there's no suppressed anger because someone didn't set a screen, or rebound, or hustle on defense, but instead the assured knowledge that on that night the team went as far as its collective abilities permitted. If the outcome is a loss, the attitude is that we lost because we were beaten, not because we didn't extend ourselves fully. The conviction that each man did his best is unshaken.

IF YOU PLAY BASKETBALL long enough, you develop a deepening respect for the game itself. When I was the Knicks representative in the players' union for nine of my ten years with the pros, the hardest thing for me to do was to think only of the union. I had to wonder whether the NBA could meet our demands without damaging the game. While I always overestimated the danger, my instinct was probably the right one: Players have an obligation to assure the game's quality—not just for reasons of self-interest, but also out of respect for what the game means to millions of fans. Point-shaving, drug scandals, and lazy players reflect badly on the sport. And once the sport is in disrepute, a player's reputation is not far behind. Ultimately, the game is what people want to see; a star player attracts customers, but it's the game that keeps them coming back.

FROM THE BENCH
Tennessee Lady Vols

Only five players can take the floor at one time, but every team needs the contributions of the sixth through twelfth man—or woman—both in practice and at the games. Here, Pat Summitt, the intense Lady Vols' coach, peers through the cheers of her bench players.

Respect for the game extends beyond
the court. Basketball is played within
communities, which support teams emotion-
ally and financially. Players such as Tim
Hardaway (left), Clyde Drexler and Hakeem
Olajuwon (opposite page) who devote
time to charities or local institutions—and in
Hakeem's case, global institutions—reflect
their concern about basketball's well-being
and its role in the community.

It's possible to drive fans away. Gratuitous violence (Latrell Sprewell assaulting
his coach), high ticket prices ($1,350 courtside tickets at Madison Square Garden),
and a perception that players care only about the money (Kevin Garnett's rejection
of a $100 million contract as insufficient) quickly put barriers between the fans and
the game. Likewise, players who are approachable and honorable draw fans to the
arena. Chamique Holdsclaw of Tennessee honors her school by her openness and
good humor. Horace Grant of Orlando consistently shows a sensitivity to kids in the
stands. Kevin Johnson of Phoenix helps children who are poor by funding a youth
developement center in his hometown of Sacramento. David Robinson gives twenty-
five tickets each home game to disadvantaged young people in San Antonio. A team
takes on something of a neighborly quality when players willingly sign autographs,
appear at various functions for free, and are aware of the power of their example on
others. By midcareer, most professional players have realized that they have an
opportunity—even more, an obligation—to fill a community role along with simply

getting rich. Sometimes players neglect this wider off-court obligation and focus only on themselves. By the time these players are ready to retire, they have little identity broader than their eroding skills. When the post-basketball world puts new demands on their character, they find that the worth of their basketball career begins to disappear behind them like footprints in a desert windstorm.

Even on the professional level, basketball is more than a business. The memories that accrue, the values learned, the human emotions shared, all bind you to the game. For most players, those memories are vivid, and those values have been internalized. They act as a counter to the materialism that surrounds the game. Once you've learned to show respect in basketball, you've probably received it as well. Then you can feel how easy it is to give even the least important person his or her due.

OPPONENTS

Magic Johnson and Larry Bird, Patrick Ewing and Hakeem Olajuwon

The volume of trash talk in the NBA can disguise the respect that most players have for their opponents. In a decade of legendary, take-no-prisoners battles, Magic Johnson and Larry Bird (above) epitomized competitive ferocity and mutual admiration. Today, despite their ferocious battles underneath the basket, NBA centers Patrick Ewing and Hakeem Olajuwon (opposite page) have a high regard for each other.

TEAMMATES

Orlando Magic, Chicago Bulls

What's the point of achieving anything in basketball if you can't share it? That's the beauty of having teammates. They know what it takes to get through a long season, to recover from a loss, to pull out a win when you're hurt and tired. Their example can force you out of lethargic play. Once good players have put on their uniforms, everything else about them—race, ethnicity, personal history, off-court style—fades into the background. It's time to play, together. That's Charles Outlaw, Mark Price, and Derek Strong of Orlando (opposite page), and Chicago's Dennis Rodman and Michael Jordan (above).

PERSPECTIVE

TEAM PLAYERS KNOW exactly where they are in relation both to their opponents and their teammates. Off the court, they come to understand the fleeting nature of victory while appreciating the breadth of support needed to achieve it. Knowledge of one's strengths and weaknesses remains a necessary but not sufficient step to success; acting on that knowledge requires perspective.

"Winning brings out the best in people who are good and the worst in people who are not," Pete Carril wrote in his memoir. You can see that pattern of behavior forming as early as high school. Some players become insufferable when they win. Others handle victory with modesty and dignity, and earn admiration for it. "When you win, don't crow; when you lose, don't cry," Arvel Popp, my high school coach, used to say. A perspective on victory comes from knowing who is responsible for it in a team sport. Never is it one player.

In 1965, I set the record for the highest number of points in an NCAA tournament game: 58. Several years later, when Austin Carr of Notre Dame scored 61 points in a game, people asked me whether I was disappointed that he had broken my record. My answer was that I didn't care, that records were made to be broken. Like batons in a relay race, they are passed from one athlete to another. In team sports, the only record that's important is the team's, not a team member's. UCLA's ten NCAA championships in twelve years and the Boston Celtics' eleven NBA championships

VICTORY

When Princeton played Providence in the 1965 NCAA East regional finals, Princeton was the underdog. But playing a near perfect team game (in the second half we hit 24 of 33 shots), Princeton won 109 to 69. That was a victory to celebrate by cutting down the net.

in thirteen years are the most impressive and important records in basketball. I predict that they'll never be broken—until they are.

BASKETBALL, perhaps above all other sports, affords a unique perspective on a fundamental moral issue of our times: the need for racial unity. Bill Russell once said that the reason he liked the game was because it was about numbers, while much else in life was politics. The implication was that given the politics of life in America, a black man would not be able to rise with his ability, because somewhere along the line racist thinking and racists acts would subvert his achievement, whereas in basketball you got the rebound or you didn't. The ball went in or it missed. There were no artificial barriers between ability and reward.

On a February evening in 1998, an organization called XNBA assembled in New York City to give its first awards to basketball players, owners, and coaches who had shaped the modern game. Bill Russell presented an award to Red Auerbach, his old coach—the man who had won nine NBA championships in ten years but had been named Coach of the Year only once. Russell got right to the point about his friendship with Red. "I never considered him a social innovator," Russell said, "but Red did things. For example, the Celtics . . . were the first team to draft a black player, a number one draft pick from one of the Negro colleges; the first team to start five black players; and the first team to hire a black coach. And I never once thought that Auerbach did that for any other reason but that he thought this was the best man for the job. And that's the only way to do things like that."

You can't play on a team with African Americans for very long and fail to recognize the stupidity of our national obsession with race. The right path is really very simple: Give respect to teammates of a different race, treat them fairly, disagree with them

RED AUERBACH
Boston Celtics, 1963

No one ever accused Red Auerbach of being a moralist. Rather, he was a master at using the smallest psychological opening to gain an advantage. And the only color Auerbach recognized was Celtics green. The color of a player's skin didn't matter, only that he could get the job done.

honestly, enjoy their friendship, explore your common humanity, share your thoughts about one another candidly, work together for a common goal, help one another achieve it. No destructive lies. No ridiculous fears. No debilitating anger.

Why, of all the places in America, is that ideal closest to being achieved on a basketball court? I believe it's because the community of a team is so close that you have to talk with one another; the travel is so constant that you have to interact with one another; the competition is so intense that you have to challenge one another; the game is so fluid that you have to depend on one another; the high and low moments are so frequent that you learn to share them; the season is so long that it brings you to mutual acceptance. That is not to say that no racists have ever survived a multiracial team experience with their prejudices intact, but my guess is that the numbers are few.

BASKETBALL SHOWS YOU how thin the line is between victory and defeat, and how we all live most of our lives in the middle, between the two. In 1970, the Knicks played the Lakers for the biggest prize in basketball, the NBA championship, and I found myself playing against my childhood heroes—Wilt Chamberlain, Elgin Baylor, and Jerry West. The series took a number of dramatic turns, with a devastating injury to Willis Reed in the fifth game and constant press comments about which was the better team, the old stars or the new upstarts. Everything came down to the seventh game.

As we approached the championship game, I began to see our campaign as something like Tolstoy's idea of war: It was not great generalship that was decisive, but rather the accidents—the unforeseen was what dictated events. Fate, in the form of Willis's torn abductor muscle, had intervened. In such circumstances, though you have prepared meticulously, you still look for a way to seize the initiative. No advantage is too small to be pounced on.

HUDDLE
Boston Celtics

The world of professional sports isn't a perfect meritocracy, but it comes close; only the best players stick around. This makes the community of basketball very different from many other communities. A team spends so much time together pursuing a common goal that it makes no sense to let an issue like race get in the way.

During the warm-ups in the Garden, West, Baylor, and Chamberlain limbered up for what they thought—absent Willis—would be their first championship together. Then Willis appeared from underneath the stands. The audience erupted in a roar as loud as Niagara Falls. The unpredictable had occurred again. The advantage shifted, and each Knick felt tremendously uplifted. DeBusschere recalls that Chamberlain, Baylor, and West stood at the other end of the court, their

LOSING THE WINNING EDGE
Willis Reed, 1970

How fragile is the boundary between winning and losing? In my first championship season, everything depended on Willis Reed. He was injured severely in the fifth game of the NBA finals against the Los Angeles Lakers and unable even to suit up in the sixth game. In a split second, our hopes for victory faded.

warm-up stopped, just watching Willis, his lips pursed in determination, take his last shots before the game's opening buzzer. If Willis's entrance had changed the momentum all by itself, the first two minutes, in which he hit his first two shots, sealed the Lakers' fate. They seemed dazed; the pressure had reached even my childhood heroes, and they were carried away in the current. Chamberlain's 45 points in the sixth game, against essentially the same team, dropped to 21 in the final. Baylor and West couldn't break out of the reversed momentum. Our team stuck together and we won.

The game could have easily gone the other way were it not for Willis's heroics, our home court advantage, or the fact that Walt Frazier's opponent, Dick Garrett, was an old teammate from college who still stood in awe of him. If any one of these countless variables had shifted, the outcome could have changed, but none of them did. When we needed to perform, we did. There would be other times in other places when it wouldn't go so well. One year later, with Willis suffering from tendonitis of the knee, we would lose in the Eastern finals to Baltimore. Two years later, a slightly different Laker team defeated us in the finals four games to one, in a series that, had a few baskets in the fourth game gone in our favor, could have stretched to seven

games—and then who knows what might have happened? Each time I think about those moments, I remember how intense they were and the perspective they gave me about how life works: about the importance of continuity, the ability to see beyond the immediate, and the fragility of balance. Awareness of this sort leads to gratitude for the bounty that life does bring you, and to a determination to live it to the fullest.

BEYOND THE GAME on the court, there is the larger world of your dealings with the public and its representatives, the press. Having the right perspective on yourself as a public figure is no easy task. The problem can crop up early in your playing career. As a high school athlete you can get some press attention and suddenly feel self-important and separate from your team. Fame, you learn, is like a rainstorm—it comes on fast and then goes just as quickly, often leaving behind a certain amount of destruction.

I always felt that the public was owed a good performance on the court, and I tried to give as close to 100 percent as possible every night, but as a pro I was never any good at the postgame interviews. Mine usually amounted to little more than restatements of the box score—besides, other teammates liked to do them. Yet I knew, and many players know, that the press is not the adversary; the first thing to understand is that most reporters are just trying to do their job. Relating to them as professionals worthy of courtesy and respect is infinitely preferable to feigning friendship or avoiding contact.

SOME OF THE VERY BEST basketball players, through their athletic accomplishments, legitimize youthful aspiration and encourage commitment. They know how hard they've worked to cultivate and extend their talents, but, with an appealing modesty, they also recognize their talents as a gift. By recognizing that they are not the sole creators of their own particular genius, these players reflect a perspective that at core can be spiritual. What comes to mind is Magic Johnson's enthusiasm. (The Greek word *enthusiasmos* means "being filled with the spirit of the gods.") Julius Erving once described what he did as literally "leaping for God." Players like this seem to have a natural understanding of the spirit. In contrast to the greed and selfishness that is too much a part of American life, and increasingly of basketball itself, they point toward another way, one influenced more by internal peace than by envy or celebrity. As the ancient Greeks understood, great athletes not only accept the ordeal of competition and the trial of strength inherent in it, but also show us a connection between what we do each day and something that is larger than we are and lasts longer than we do.

GAME SEVEN
Willis Appears

The Knicks were already on the floor when Willis made his appearance. With every step he took, the crowd, already on its feet, roared louder. It was the emotional peak of a remarkable season. "I'd like to tell people that it was Red Holzman's strategy for me to come out late and then hit the first two shots," Willis told *The New York Times*. "But the problem was the doctor needed more time than he thought for the injection."

THE STEAL

One errant pass, one shot that bounces off the rim, and a game (a team, your life) can be changed. Take the memorable seventh-game finish during the 1965 Eastern Division finals between the Celtics and the Philadelphia 76ers. The Sixers, behind by 1 point, had the ball with 5 seconds to go. Plenty of time to get a good shot and win the game. Hal Greer inbounded the ball, but streaking between him and Chet Walker (25), the intended receiver, was John Havlicek. I can still hear Johnny Most, the Celtics announcer, screaming in his foghorn voice, "Havlicek stole the ball! Havlicek stole the ball!" A lucky play by a hustling Hondo? Maybe, but as Bill Russell likes to say, "Hustle is talent."

COURAGE

WHEN I WAS FOURTEEN and a freshman in high school, I already stood 6 feet 3 and weighed 165 pounds. Despite my size, I didn't go out for the football team; it was basketball I loved. The high school coach, who coached both sports but preferred football, suspected I was afraid of getting hurt. After I made the varsity basketball team that year, he decided to test my courage. During Christmas break, before the drills of official practice began, he arranged a boxing match between me and a visiting alumnus, an all-American college football player who was two inches taller and some fifty pounds heavier than I was. I took a pounding, but because I didn't back down I think I proved something to the coach.

Courage in sports means, in the simplest terms, giving 100 percent for your team. In basketball, if there's a loose ball, you dive for it; forget that the floor is hardwood. If you go for a rebound and get elbowed in the face, make sure that next time you go back even harder. If you're playing tough defense and the man you're guarding takes you into a screen set by a burly forward, fight over the screen. If you set a screen and a big forward is about to run into you with all the force of a linebacker, take the hit. Every time I see Patrick Ewing take the charge by placing his body in front of a 6-feet-9 240-pound forward going full speed for the basket, I want to hug him in admiration.

OLD WARRIORS
Patrick Ewing, Bill Cartwright

When he played for the Bulls, center Bill Cartwright (24) was the epitome of a smart player who was also unafraid to throw his body around. He'd often start bumping his opponent as soon as the opponent crossed the half-court line, just to deny him good position. Patrick Ewing (33), his former Knicks teammate, has stood for a decade on the court in Madison Square Garden like a midtown Manhattan skyscraper, taking an enormous amount of physical abuse in the Knicks' hard-nosed defensive scheme.

It's worth emphasizing that courage is not the same thing as fearlessness. It means accepting and then overcoming fear—fear of injury, of failing, of looking bad, of relinquishing excuses.

In December of my rookie year, I was playing guard against Boston, but I was too slow, particularly on defense. We were applying a full-court press. I picked up my man with the ball at the inbounds baseline. Moving my feet like a water spider gliding over the water's surface, I tried to pressure him toward the sidelines. Just past the center court line, Wayne Embry, a towering 260-pound backup center, set a blindside screen. I crashed into him and slumped to the floor as if I'd run into a brick wall. At that moment, courage meant shaking off the hurt and embarrassment and finding my man again. (If you're slow, sometimes courage is your last resource!)

Occasionally during my ten years in the league, I would be so badly injured that I couldn't play for a couple of games. I'd sit in street clothes on the bench, watching giants run like gazelles and jump like ballet dancers. I'd see—and hear—the bruising contact when one player boxed out another for rebounds; I'd watch all the defensive hacking and clawing, the tough fouls on a drive. Each time I'd have the same reaction: I play out there?

You can see the most visceral kind of courage in basketball when sick or injured players stay in the game for the good of the team. When a reporter asked the English runner David Moorcroft why he had never dropped out of a race even in the worst of circumstances, he replied, "I think that once you do, you've given yourself an option for the future." There isn't a great basketball player who hasn't played with a muscle pull, a sprained knee or ankle, a sore back, contusions, a cold, the flu, or an upset stomach. Later in the hotel room, when the chills get you,

MICHAEL BATTLES THE BUG
Bulls vs. Jazz, 1997

The fifth game of the 1997 NBA finals against the Utah Jazz was yet another one of the legendary performances in Michael Jordan's career. Ill with the flu and a high fever, he dragged himself out of bed, overcoming his weakened state because his team needed him. A year later, in the sixth game of the finals against the same team, it was Scottie Pippen who, with his back in painful spasms, refused to quit.

you wonder whether you were crazy, but in the locker room before the game that's one question you don't ask yourself.

In that seventh game of the 1970 finals against Los Angeles the pain in Willis Reed's leg was so bad that he could hardly walk. In 1997, Michael Jordan was running a fever of 102 in the fifth game of the finals against the Utah Jazz, but he played anyway. He wasn't afraid of looking bad because of a below-par performance. He wasn't afraid of permanent damage to his health. And he wasn't willing to hold himself back. Calling upon some inner reserve of strength, he gave it everything he had: 38 points, 7 rebounds, and 5 assists.

Larry Bird's last seasons in the NBA are a classic example of this kind of courage. After nine years of wear and tear, his back was giving him a lot of trouble. Each time he left the locker room, Bird moved as if he were disabled, but when he got to the hardwood, out there before the crowd, something happened to him. "It was as if he'd been given a new back," former Celtics CEO Dave Gavitt told me at a Hall of Fame induction ceremony. "He didn't seem to realize he was in pain until the competition was behind him." When Bird finished the 1991–92 season, the prognosis was grim; his body had finally worn out. His contract contained a two-year option for $4.5 million a year, which would automatically take effect on August 15 if he didn't notify the club of his retirement. On August 12, Bird went to see Gavitt and announced that he was going to retire. Gavitt, aware of the August 15 deadline and of all the years of dedicated service Larry had given the Celtics, asked him whether he wanted a few more days to think it over. "I know what day this is," Bird replied. "If I'm not going to play and know I can't play, I'm not going to take the money. I'm not going to take one cent I don't earn."

Sometimes the motivation to play while you're in pain is not simply victory but an urge to prove yourself to your peers. During my second season in

"LARRY LEGEND"

No one knows when Larry Bird realized that his bad back would not get better. But whenever he fell to his knees in excruciating pain in his last year in the league, teammates and opponents alike showed their concern. When a great player goes down, it's like a giant redwood crashing onto the forest floor.

the NBA, I was a guard and still not performing up to my expectations. In January, Cazzie Russell, a Knicks starting forward, broke his ankle, and Red Holzman had me take his place. It was my big chance. A few days later, we flew into San Diego for a game. I began feeling ill shortly after we arrived at the motel, and by the time I reached the locker room I was nauseated. When the game began, I was still sick, and after a few times up and down the floor, I went over to the bench during a time-out and vomited into a bucket. We were shorthanded that night, and I was determined not to come out of the game. Several times during free throws, I held the basket pole and dry-heaved. I kept telling myself, "Put it out of your mind. Keep playing." The other players were laughing, but I have no doubt that every one of them understood what was going on in my head.

SHOOTING INVOLVES its own kind of subtle courage. When all the money is on the line, a brave player wants the ball. He is willing to stare defeat down. His confidence builds with the pressure. The standing joke on many teams is about the scorer who wants the ball for three quarters but can't be found at crunch time. Technically his shooting is perfect, but his fear of failure is too great.

If you're a shooter and you start missing, you have to keep taking your open shots. This is no small thing. Missing makes some players nervous. They begin to hesitate, consciously or subconsciously. Taking another shot is a torture instead of an opportunity, so they stop shooting altogether. The great player is willing to keep trying.

For most of my years with the Knicks, all five starters would take the shot. When one of us missed, the others never complained, never blamed. We were a team. We understood this, but sometimes the crowd didn't. In 1971, in the seventh game of the Eastern playoff against Baltimore, the score was Baltimore 93, New York 91, with about ten seconds left on the clock. On a broken play for Walt Frazier, I got the ball with four seconds to go and only the baseline open. I took two dribbles and then the shot, but Wes Unseld, the Baltimore center, got a piece of it, and the ball hit

On the foul line with the game in the balance, your knees bent, elbow under the ball, you concentrate on the rim, shoot, and follow through. On a children's TV show, I once shot a foul with my eyes closed in order to demonstrate that practice makes perfect, and it went in. But in the NBA, I always kept my eyes open.

the side of the backboard, ending our dreams of a second straight championship. To this day (most recently on a 1998 visit to the floor of the American Stock Exchange), perfect strangers ask me, "Why'd you miss that shot back in '71 against Baltimore?"

The foul line is the place where a player is most exposed. You're there all alone. No one is guarding you. There are no excuses. The only thing that defeats you is pressure and a lack of courage. In 1968, in a game against Boston, I was fouled during the last minute and a half, with the Knicks 1 point ahead. If I hit both foul shots, we'd probably win; if I missed, we could lose. This was one of the few games early in my career when the coach had put me in at crunch time. I wasn't a starter, and in that game I was shooting 1 for 10 from the field. Needless to say, I felt the tension rising. As I went to the line, the ref compounded it by handing me the ball and saying, "Now we'll see what you're made of." Despite the warm words, I sank both shots.

A similar situation occurred during a Sunday game in the 1997 NBA finals between Utah and Chicago. Utah Jazz forward Karl Malone—nicknamed the Mailman,

When you're playing away from home, the crowd in the arena can be remarkably cruel in its attempts to intimidate you, and it would be a mistake to expect anything else but grief from them. The great foul shooters, finding some inner calm, can block out the harassment and get the job done.

because he always seems to deliver in the clutch—missed two free throws with seconds to go in the game. Utah lost. Much was made of Scottie Pippen's words to Malone before his shots: "Hey, Karl, the mailman don't deliver on Sunday." But the real story was what happened afterward. Many players would have offered some excuse for the misses—maybe even blaming it on Pippen's attempt at psyching. Not Malone. He took full responsibility. He missed, next time he'd do better. Another kind of courage.

THERE HAVE BEEN TIMES when basketball players have shown a courage that many working people can understand. In the early years of the NBA, the players had no benefits and were paid poorly. But a small group of the players decided to form a union to get themselves out of third-rate hotels on the road and, more important, establish a pension system and health coverage. The owners ignored them until the 1964 All-Star Game, when the players refused to play until the owners recognized the union. The owners threatened to fire them, but the players stood firm: No recognition of the union, no All-Star game. In the locker room, these All-Stars were well aware that they were acting on behalf of every other professional basketball player. The owners relented, and the All-Star game took place that night. It was a familiar story, one that had already been played out in many industries in America. For me, it reinforces the idea that with a little courage, even if you wield little power individually, you can make great things happen when you join forces.

I N   B A S K E T B A L L ,   just facing the crowd sometimes takes courage. The crowd intimidates and wears you down. It is unforgiving. It can inflict personal pain, as it did to me in my rookie year. The fans in New York expected nothing less than immediate stardom from me, and when it didn't happen they became hostile. After the first ten or so games, people would start booing whenever my name was mentioned. A few of the unrulier fans would throw things at me as I left the floor. On the street, strangers frequently greeted me with ridicule. Every night that I went into the arena was a night of potential embarrassment before the home crowd. It was as if I'd been put in the ring with the heavyweight champion and couldn't get away. But by the end of the year, I had gained confidence by the sheer act of persevering.

By contrast, I found it easy to steel myself against the derision of crowds away from home. Most are merciless toward the opposing team. The air is filled with boos and catcalls. To the crowd, the opposing players are the enemy. Their humanity is denied; in the early years of the league, black players had to face a constant barrage of racist epithets. Some players get angry at the fans who sit right behind the visitors' bench in many arenas and shout obscenities or make loud and uncomplimentary remarks about a player's ability, or his looks, or his family pedigree. Some players get rattled when the crowd stands and waves behind the backboard in an attempt to distract them. For most, though, this kind of audience hostility toward the visiting team is nothing new. It brings back memories of high school games and summer leagues, when the slightest disagreement with a call might precipitate a fight or at least a lot of sounding off, and the audience occasionally became menacing. Once you've been through those adolescent wars, the away-from-home crowds in the pros can seem like a piece of cake.

THE FANS

When an NBA team wins on the road, you often hear the winning players talk about taking the fans out of the game with a solid spurt of play. Obviously, the fans aren't really in the game, but their role in the outcome is real, and you're always aware of it. There's no question that the home arena can provide a tremendous boost, inspiring the team to rally when it's behind or turn a tight game into a blowout. When that happens, your previous errors are generally forgiven. For one night, at least, you're the toast of the town.

HITTING THE DECK

Dennis Rodman, Larry Bird

BILL BRADLEY

Not every pro dives after a loose ball, even those who make millions of dollars a year. Then there are people like Dennis Rodman (above), who gets as much horizontal air as he does vertical. The perils of diving into the stands don't deter him. His job is to get the ball for his teammates. Larry Bird (opposite page) had every reason not to dive after a loose ball that came his way: He was a star, and one with a bad back at that. But he never hesitated; he couldn't play any other way. He was willing to risk it all every night. He had the courage to lead by example.

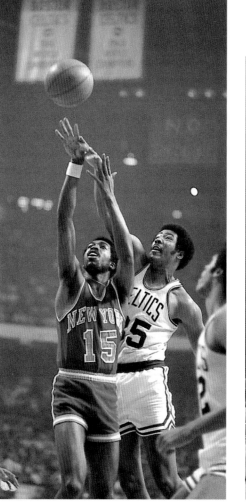

THE BUZZER BEATERS

The clock is ticking down, the score is tight. This is the critical time in many games, yet this is the time when some players don't seem to want the ball. They stop moving, preferring to watch one or another of their teammates maneuver for the last shot. On my Knicks teams, Dave DeBusschere (22), Walt Frazier (10), Earl Monroe (15), and Jerry Lucas (32) never hesitated to take the open shot when the game was on the line. Often enough, the ball went in.

LEADERSHIP

LEADERSHIP MEANS getting people to think, believe, see, and do what they might not have without you. It means possessing the vision to set the right goal and the decisiveness to pursue it single-mindedly. It means being aware of the fears and anxieties felt by those you lead even as you urge them to overcome those fears. It can appear in a speech before hundreds of people or in a dialogue with one other person—or simply by example.

To the Bulls' Phil Jackson, the key leadership function for a coach in the pros is getting the players to commit to something bigger than themselves. In the simplest sense, winning is the purpose of playing, but to achieve that end a coach frequently has to create a context larger than the immediate game. At each level I played, the desire to win was a reflection of a deeper desire: In my small-town high school, the motivation was to beat the big city schools; in college, the challenge was for a group of athletes who were primarily students to beat the best in the NCAA; in the pros, the larger purpose was to show that a team without a dominant star could win the NBA title. Pete Carril's idea of leadership was to ask his players to give a little more than they thought they were capable of giving and by so doing achieve a bit more than they were capable of achieving. That's why Princeton on occasion became a giant killer.

A wise coach doesn't do all the talking. Sometimes, with the right group, he'll let the team

HANK IBA

There was never any doubt who was leading a Hank Iba team. In his raspy voice, he would bark orders as if he were a drill sergeant. Iba's players could be confident that whatever the game circumstances they would be prepared. Iba would have anticipated the moment, devised a strategy to deal with it, and made sure you had practiced it long before the moment arrived.

Princeton coach Pete Carril (left) has
observed that "a pass is not a pass when
it is made after you've tried to do everything else" and that "hardly any players
play to lose—only a few play to win."
In the ego-driven environment of the
NBA, Chicago Bulls coach Phil Jackson
(opposite page) respects each of his players
as individuals but emphasizes the need for
selfless behavior and constant improvement
within a community of players.

members put pressure on players who are problem children. In 1994, the Bulls, without
Michael Jordan, were playing the Knicks for the Eastern Conference semifinals. In the
last seconds of a close game three, Jackson called the game-deciding play, with Toni
Kukoc rather than Scottie Pippen as the shooter. An angered Pippen took himself out
of the game. Kukoc hit the shot and the Bulls won, but Pippen's highly visible act of
insubordination posed an immediate challenge for Jackson. Phil declined to come
down hard on Pippen in his postgame interview. In the locker room, however, he
closed the door, announced that he thought the team had something to say to Pippen,
and then left the room. Bill Cartwright, a quintessential team player who was in the
final year of his career, was so upset that he was close to tears as he asked Pippen how
he could have let the team down after all they had sacrificed for as a group throughout
the year. Other players chimed in along similar lines. Pippen, man enough to see his
error, apologized on the spot, and in the next game he was back contributing to the
Bulls' performance. If Phil himself had confronted Scottie, the result might not have
been as positive; by harnessing the team to do his work, he was more effective.

Coaches who seek the media limelight risk irritating their star players, and the
results can be counterproductive: Pouting stars rarely win big games. Coaches who

use the media to criticize their players also often live to regret it. Red Holzman was a master in dealing with the press. For him, the only thing that counted was what happened on the floor: He knew that as far as the public was concerned, if the team won, he was a success; if it lost, he was a failure. This insight, combined with his natural modesty and fierce desire to win, produced a postgame demeanor that was, well, unnewsworthy. He never criticized a player. He spoke in truisms that nevertheless underlined his basic principles: All his players were talented; defense was the key; teamwork paid off; only victory was acceptable. Period, end of interview. Red confined his criticism of our play to the locker room, where it belonged.

Above all, the coach who exercises leadership communicates clearly to the players what they have to do. It's not unlike military training: A commando operation succeeds because each person has a particular assignment and knows what it is in precise detail. The same is true of basketball, but many coaches either burden their players with an overly complicated offense or they don't suggest any structure to the offense at all. You can be a freewheeling practice coach, like Princeton's Van Breda Kolff, or a structured practice coach, like Hank Iba, but in each case you have to make sure that every player knows what you want. If you have prepared well enough, events in the game can't rattle you. I love to see a team that's ready when the opponent tries a full-court press. That readiness comes only with hours of practice in which each player knows where to go and what to do in order to break the opponent's press. Picking it apart with precision passes and cuts often leads to easy baskets. It takes only a few such responses before the team that's doing the pressing retreats from further embarrassment.

Another example of leadership through preparation is getting your team ready for the last-second shot. In the 1998 NCAA tournament, Valparaiso trailed the University of Mississippi by 2 and had the ball out of bounds at the opposite end of the floor. Valparaiso's Jamie Sykes threw a long pass to teammate Bill Jenkins at the top of the key. Jenkins leaped, caught the ball in midair, and seemingly without pausing

to look, flicked it to his left—to Bryce Drew, who shot behind the 3-point line and made the basket, giving Valparaiso the victory. Afterward, both coach and players made the point that the team had rehearsed that particular play all season but had never had a chance to use it until the most important game of the year.

Tactics are not everything; sometimes a coach needs to provide personal leadership. In 1982, Georgetown played the University of North Carolina for the NCAA championship. It was a matchup featuring two of the NCAA's greatest players that year: Georgetown's Patrick Ewing and North Carolina's James Worthy. It was also a matchup of two great coaches: Dean Smith of North Carolina and John Thompson of Georgetown. The game was hard fought and came down to the last seconds. North Carolina went ahead by 1 with eighteen seconds to go on a jump shot by a freshman named Michael Jordan. Georgetown took possession of the ball with

LEADERSHIP STYLES
Larry Bird, Red Holzman, Lenny Wilkens

Larry Bird (left) has used his stature as one of the NBA's greatest players and his style of calm intensity to communicate confidence to the rising Indiana Pacers. Red Holzman (center) and Lenny Wilkens (right) are models of successful coaches who demonstrate that showmanship has little to do with leadership.

plenty of time to make the winning basket. Then—inexplicably, in one of those very human moments on the court—Fred Brown, a Georgetown guard, mistook James Worthy for a teammate and threw a pass directly into Worthy's hands.

Georgetown's dream of a championship disappeared. The team was devastated. The fans were in shock. All eyes were on Brown. He had committed a blunder that would be with him for the rest of his life. Thompson understood this, and putting aside his disappointment he wrapped the young player in a bear hug, whispering reassurance in his ear. It was one of the most moving gestures I have ever witnessed on a basketball court. It spoke volumes about Thompson's relationship to his players, about his most fundamental values, about his excellence as a leader. Billy Packer, the great CBS basketball broadcaster and former star at Wake Forest, recalls seeing a player—Robert "Tractor" Traylor of the University of Michigan—provide similar extraordinary leadership late in the 1997-98 season, when teammate Robbie Reid, a guard who had transferred to Michigan from Brigham Young that year, missed the last-second shot against Michigan State in a Big Ten conference game. The failure seemed emblematic of Reid's year at Michigan up to that point: He had been a disappointment. Instead of disparaging him, Traylor, all 300 pounds of him, put his arms around his dejected teammate and offered the right words of encouragement. Reid went on to play exceptionally well in the remaining games, and together with Traylor, he powered Michigan to victory in the first Big Ten postseason tournament.

Watching the NCAA Final Four games in 1998, I felt that while the country's best players might not be on the floor, the players that "fit together best" (as Red Auerbach puts it) were there; in other words, the country's best teams were on the floor. Time and time again, you saw the leadership rotating, like the lead goose flying in a V formation. In Stanford's semifinal overtime game against the University of Kentucky, a different player responded at each critical moment. In the last minutes three players—Arthur Lee, Peter Sauer, and Ryan Mendez—hit 3-point shots, two others got important rebounds, and everyone on coach Mike Montgomery's team played great defense. Stanford lost, but each player had truly done his best. Kentucky played Utah in the final, and it was the same story: Different players on both teams sparked their team's momentum at different times in the game. At one point, Kentucky's Heshimu Evans entered as a substitute and went straight to the point of the V, contributing significantly to Kentucky's eventual victory. Once you've seen such broad-based leadership in basketball, you can better appreciate the value of giving a cross-section of people in

DIGNITY IN CATASTROPHE
1982 NCAA Championship

Georgetown's John Thompson has always coached his teams to play hard and win: "If you want to have a lot of friends, lose." Yet in his most agonizing loss, the 1982 NCAA championship against North Carolina, he showed us that compassion is more important than victory.

any organization the opportunity to assume responsibility. You learn that within each of us is the ability to excel, even, or perhaps especially, in times of crisis.

There are also players who lead during a game simply by virtue of their self-confidence. Dean Smith has remarked that often the player who provides the emotional leadership is not necessarily the team's best player but the one who is held in the greatest respect by the team. When the best player is also the most respected, such as Isiah Thomas, Larry Bird, or the incomparable Michael Jordan, a different dynamic takes over. The best player can then lead by example, contributing more than anyone else to the effort and at the same time spurring teammates to outdo themselves. Oscar Robertson, one of the all-time great NBA stars, once told me that the mark of a truly excellent player is that he makes the worst player on his team into a good one.

SPORTS ARE AN IMPORTANT part of many people's lives, both as pursuit and as pastime. They can influence people in subtle ways, helping shape their ideas about how life works and about what is acceptable behavior. When professional baseball and basketball decided on racial desegregation in the late 1940s and early 1950s, it had a far-reaching impact on society. Once the taboo of separateness was challenged on the fields of millions of Americans' dreams, children began to ask their parents questions and adults increasingly found the old ways indefensible. What had seemed impossible began to change. If desegregation worked in sports, why shouldn't it work in the rest of American life? The heroes in this racial drama are well known: Branch Rickey of the Brooklyn Dodgers, Bill Veeck of the Cleveland Indians, Ned Irish of the New York Knicks—all of them executives who saw the future; Jackie Robinson, Larry Doby, Nat "Sweetwater" Clifton—black players who lived the experience and in so doing exposed the hollowness and falseness of racial stereotypes.

BREAKING BARRIERS

Breaking the NBA's color barrier required the willingness of players like Earl Lloyd of the Syracuse Nationals and Nat "Sweetwater" Clifton (pictured) to step out first, knowing they would have to endure the inevitable racial slurs.

BILL BRADLEY

What is not so well known are the conflicts that had to be resolved among the players. When Rickey announced that Jackie Robinson was joining the Dodgers, tension quickly rose in the clubhouse, a place that cherishes conformity and rarely rewards dissent. A wholesale defection from Rickey's dream seemed to be in the making: Several players drew up a petition stating their refusal to play with Robinson. Many of the players signed it; a significant exception was Pee Wee Reese, the team's shortstop and captain. Reese, a white Kentuckian, would later make a point of putting his arm around Robinson's shoulder when fans heckled him for being who he was. Reese's splendid act of leadership made a powerful statement, with repercussions across the nation as well as within his team.

A much subtler revolution began in 1972 with the passage of Title IX, which required high schools and colleges to provide women with access to athletic facilities equal to those for men. By 1997–98, women's basketball reached a new level of public acceptance. The NCAA champion Tennessee Lady Vols averaged attendance of over 14,000 at all their home games. At Southwest Missouri State University in Springfield, a town of fewer than 150,000 people, the average game attendance was nearly 8,000. Through the 1980s, women players such as Carol Blazejowski, Nancy Lieberman, Cheryl Miller, Teresa Edwards, and Ann Meyers showed that they were world-class athletes, but after college there were few places they could continue to play. Then, in 1997, the women's professional leagues took off. The WNBA and ABL games attracted a wide attendance; both leagues were televised. Players such as Rebecca Lobo, Lisa Leslie, and Cynthia Cooper became media stars. Advertisers began using the better players in commercials for shoes, cars, and credit cards. WNBA player Jamila Wideman was even featured on the Nike website. It had been a long, hard battle, and women basketball players were finally accorded recognition and respect.

CLEARING ANOTHER HURDLE
Women's Basketball Takes Off

It took an act of Congress for women to get access to adequate facilities and coaching, but now all across America they learn the values of the game. The quality of their play has proved that they belong on the court, and thousands of fans are turning out to watch their favorite female stars.

Many different kinds of leadership brought women's basketball to its current place. There were the small colleges, such as Immaculata, Old Dominion, and Louisiana Tech, which made early and significant commitments to women's basketball. There were the coaches—Pat Summitt of Tennessee, Theresa Grentz of Illinois, Tara VanDerveer of Stanford, Geno Auriemma of Connecticut, and countless others—who loved the game and believed that the values it taught were gender-blind and that the excitement the women's game could generate was at least as great as

that created by the men. There were the high school and college athletic directors who embraced Title IX as an opportunity and opened up gym space, practice fields, and weight rooms. There is even a place in the story for NBA commissioner David Stern, who decided to put the league's marketing muscle behind the WNBA. But among the most effective were those mothers and fathers across America who saw the common sense of opening sports to women and wanted their daughters to have the same chances as their sons to experience the game.

The great leaders in basketball have never been afraid of change and they have led from the strength of their own convictions. And, above all, they have brought out the best in the people they lead.

ROLE MODELS

Before the success of the WNBA and the ABL, great college players like Nancy Lieberman (oppposite page) and Cheryl Miller (left) had to go to Europe or Japan to continue playing. Nowadays, players like Michele Timms (center) and Rebecca Lobo (right) have a solid American audience for their games.

LEADING ON THE COURT

Bill Russell and Bob Cousy, Robert Traylor, Isiah Thomas

Every team needs a floor leader, and for a while the Boston Celtics had two (opposite page). On offense, Bob Cousy (14) was the maestro of the team's fast break; on defense, Bill Russell was a tactician without peer, whose intelligence and playing skills led to his appointment as player-coach of the Celtics in 1966. When the Detroit Pistons ruled the NBA in 1989 and 1990, there was never any question as to who directed traffic on the floor: Isiah Thomas (right). Sometimes players can surprise you by picking unexpected moments to lead. At Michigan State, Robert "Tractor" Traylor (left) impressed me with a generous gesture of support for his teammate Robbie Reid after a particularly bad loss.

RESPONSIBILITY

THE FIRST DAY OF practice always tells the story about which players have taken physical conditioning seriously in the off-season. In basketball, if you can't run, you can't play. If you haven't been running for two months before the first practice, you haven't fulfilled your responsibility to the team. Red Holzman's rule was that the Knicks were all adults, that we knew we made our living with our bodies, and that if we couldn't keep them in condition we were hurting not just ourselves but the team. He also said, by way of threatening afterthought, "And then don't expect to get playing time." It was up to each of us to stay in condition. Occasionally someone would report to training camp out of shape. Our response would be like that of sharks going after a piece of bloody meat. We would run over, around, and past the laggard until he got the message.

Players who want to last in the NBA must take serious care of themselves. Karl Malone wants to play well past the age when most players retire, so he works out year-round. He lifts weights, runs on the StairMaster, stretches nearly every day. Dennis Rodman is another player who prides himself on his physical shape. When he runs down the floor with his knees kicking high, as if he were a sprinter, he is flaunting his conditioning. The store of energy from a well-honed body also shows in his persistence as a rebounder.

While some young athletes think of themselves as invincible, even immortal, and consequently abuse

HITTING THE WEIGHTS
Mark Price

You don't become the NBA's all-time leader in free-throw percentage (.907) unless you're willing to work at it—say, five hundred shots a day in the off-season, one hundred in season. Orlando's Mark Price has embraced the obligation and knows that staying fit is one reason he has been able to play in the league for more than ten years.

VALUES OF THE GAME

119

their bodies with drugs or alcohol, most professional players recognize the gift of time they've been given. Walt Frazier's public image included mink coats, wide-brimmed hats, luxurious cars, beautiful women. The image was a more or less accurate picture of his public lifestyle, but no one on the Knicks was in better condition. Walt, too, worked out year-round. He was a health food advocate before it was cool to be one. He always got plenty of rest. His pride—amounting to a kind of obsession with looking good and a determination never to be embarrassed on the court—and his desire to perform at levels that few had ever reached required that his body function like a well-oiled machine.

STYLE—AND SUBSTANCE
Walt "Clyde" Frazier

If any player ever gave the impression that he spent much of his free time running around town, it was Clyde. He was not unknown in New York's hot spots. But Frazier spent much more of his time running around the gym. He was a superb athlete who took superb care of himself.

By the time most players reach the pros, they've shot a basketball a million times. To stay there they know they have to shoot a million more. Chris Mullin of the Pacers, with two assistants feeding him balls, regularly takes an incredible one thousand shots in a normal one-hour practice. In 1984, Larry Bird was the league MVP and the leader of the world-champion Boston Celtics. Shortly after the celebrations ended, he went home to French Lick, Indiana. All summer he lifted weights in the morning and for hours every afternoon went to a gym, often alone, and shot baskets. Magic Johnson once said of Larry Bird, "To most players, basketball is a job. To Larry, it was life." One could say the same thing about Magic—or Rick Barry or Jerry West, Nate Archibald or George Gervin, Dave Cowens or George Mikan.

Hubie Brown became an assistant coach for the Milwaukee Bucks in 1972. Kareem Abdul-Jabbar was the team's center. Brown, eager to show the coaching staff how conscientious he was, arrived at practice on the first day of training camp one and a half hours before it was scheduled to begin. To his astonishment, Kareem, the league MVP for the previous two seasons, was already on the floor practicing, shooting skyhook after skyhook, perfecting his graceful release, grooving his rhythm—look at the basket, step left, cradle the ball, right leg up, swing the right arm high, release, follow through— putting in the time as if he were a sophomore in high school. To Kareem, this effort at skill development was just part of being a champion. An aspect of his daily routine involved shooting the hook with a rebounding ring inside the rim, thereby shrinking the space available for a successful shot. When he removed the ring after the thirty-day training period, he said that he felt as if he were shooting the ball into the ocean.

It seems elementary, but abiding by the team rules is another responsibility. Kids who grow up in a chaotic environment often have little sense of time, so arriving at practice at a scheduled hour becomes a major task. The coach who gets across the importance of punctuality introduces order into many a young life. On Red Holzman's teams, there were few rules, but they were rigid. His attitude was "No excuses—none!" If you weren't on the bus at the designated time, it left without you.

If you didn't make the plane, you paid your own way. If you were late for practice, even two minutes late, you were fined. The result was that most of us turned up early. Even if you were late because of circumstances clearly beyond your control, you got no sympathy or credit. "Sure, Bill, I know your mother's cousin called with an emergency that your mother's nephew couldn't take care of," Holzman used to say, "and it rained on the highway and made it slick, after the earthquake damaged the bridge, but still you're fined." He smiled and I paid up.

C O N D I T I O N I N G, skill development, and following the rules are readily understandable to most players. A player's responsibilities to the team are more subtle. No player can be a scorer, dribbler, rebounder, and passer to the degree that he or she chooses. The coach has to be clear about your role, but only you can then fill it. You have to fit your talents into the game plan.

Frequently, for the benefit of the team, you have to sacrifice what you would like to do on the court. Scoring 12 points a game and playing your role on a winning team is better than scoring 20 points a game on a losing team. For you to get those 20 points would require a change in team balance and make victory less likely.

In college, I did what I wanted on the court, following my creative impulses to score and generate team movement. In the pros, I had to adjust to playing a defined role. My job was to hit the open shot, move without the ball, push it up the court quickly, pass to the open man, keep my man from getting rebounds, constantly overplay him on defense, and help out if a teammate lost his own man.

Satch Sanders understood that his role on the Boston Celtics of the 1960s was to play tough defense and help rebound, not score. Bob Gross on the 1977 NBA champion Portland Trail Blazers knew that his role was

SKY KING
Kareem Abdul-Jabbar

Kareem played as if he were a descendant of African royalty who knew things the rest of us couldn't know. His grace masked his intensity as a competitor, and underlying every aspect of his game was a ferocious work ethic. He took it upon himself, quietly, to groove his patented sky hook with countless hours of practice.

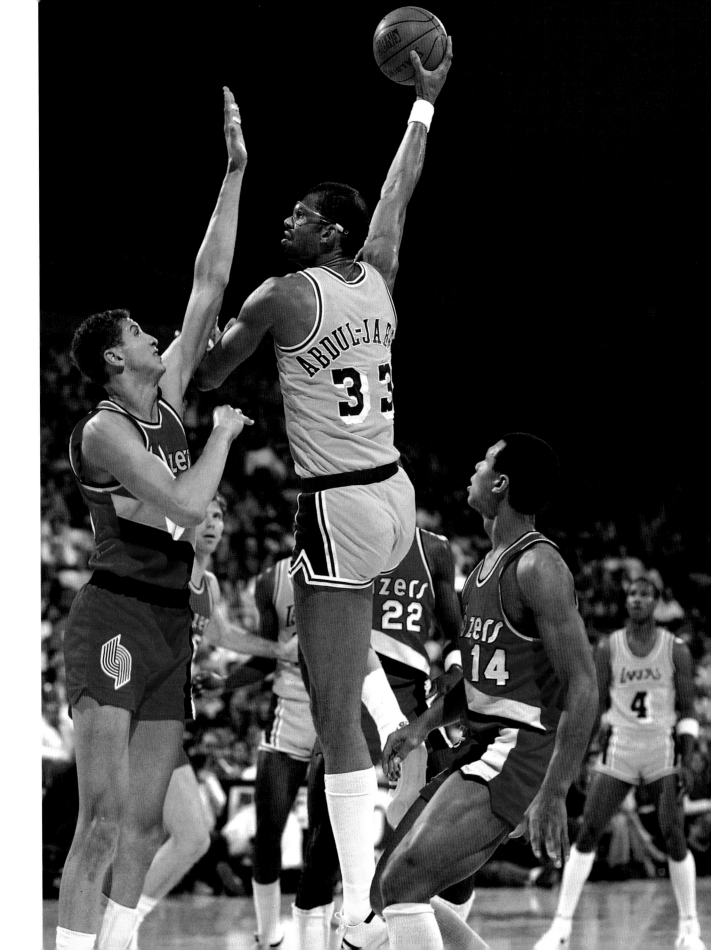

On and off the floor, certain players take responsibility for setting the tone of team behavior. Dave DeBusschere (left) and Willis Reed (right) played that role when I was on the Knicks. The team meshed so well because the rest of us accepted their leadership while contributing in our own ways to team coherence.

to move without the ball in order to create lanes for passes from Bill Walton to him; to make passes to the guards and lobs to Walton; to set screens against the opposing team's forwards and guards in order to free up his teammates Maurice Lucas or Lionel Hollins. Jeff Hornacek of the Utah Jazz plays a similar role, throwing his body in front of forwards to draw the charge, screening away to free up a teammate, moving to the open spot for the shot. Probably neither Sanders nor Gross nor Hornacek will ever make the Hall of Fame, but all three assumed responsibility for their roles and were thus absolutely essential to their teams' victories.

Each player contributes to the team's off-court chemistry, too, and the results are vital to success. Every team has its subtle personality balance, its mixture of humor and jealousy, its pecking order and center of gravity. On the Knicks, Willis Reed was the boss, the captain. He was the protector during the games and the leader in practice. Everyone acknowledged this. DeBusschere was the other pillar of strength. The rest of us operated within the structure Willis and Dave established. There was a balance of talents and personalities. Dick Barnett was the droll observer of life, able to cut players or celebrities in the news down to size. Earl Monroe provided the ballast that came from a quiet dignity and a willingness to listen to a teammate's problems. Jerry Lucas, using his prodigious memory, kept score in the yearlong poker game on the road, tabulating who owed what to whom at a particular moment in the year and making sure that money never came between teammates. My off-court role sometimes involved taking aside a white rookie with a residue of resentment for black players and telling him that that's not how we did things on the Knicks.

People on a meshed team will help each other personally. They don't necessarily share their innermost thoughts, but when one man is down psychologically, another picks him up. A group of self-absorbed soloists, on the other hand, never ceases its internal competition.

When Wilt Chamberlain joined Los Angeles in 1968, Elgin Baylor was the verbal leader off court. He was the one who awarded the nicknames and made the jokes on the bus. Wilt's arrival presented him with a challenge, because Wilt sought preeminence in repartee as well as in basketball statistics. In situations that should have been funny, Wilt and Elgin ended up arguing. No general manager can determine off-court personality roles. They just happen.

In 1982 Moses Malone, an established pro of the first order, joined the Philadelphia 76ers. He had been the NBA MVP two times. The press speculated that with his addition to the team, the brilliant Philadelphia forward Julius Erving might win his first championship. The big "if" was whether the new team would mesh.

Dr. J had been there before. In 1977, the 76ers had had a very good chance to win the NBA title, but their team dynamics collapsed around them in the finals against the Portland Trail Blazers. When Dr. J wanted to pass, no one moved to the open spot to receive it. When Dr. J moved without the ball, no one hit him with a pass at a place where he had room to "operate." The Sixers played as if they were in parallel worlds, equidistant from one another, guaranteed never to touch. I felt that the core of the problem was an apparent conflict between forward George McGinnis and Dr. J. A prolific scorer himself, McGinnis seemed to want equal billing. This

Each player has to recognize and accept his duty to the team. In Moses Malone's (2) case, it meant a willingness to turn down his lamp so as not to try to outshine Julius Erving (6). The gentlemanly Dr. J was more than happy to share the limelight, and a championship, with Moses.

off-court problem became an on-court one. Now I wondered whether the addition of Moses Malone would be a replay of that situation. But to the relief of coach Billy Cunningham and general manager Pat Williams, Malone asserted at the opening press conference that the Sixers were Dr. J's team and that he was there to help the forward win his first title. He proceeded to do just that, unselfishly playing his heart out the entire season, rebounding relentlessly, and adding the missing ingredient to a good Philadelphia team that became a championship Philadelphia team.

THE PART OF PERSONAL responsibility that's least appreciated is mental preparation. Every player has a different approach. For some, the pregame ritual consists of shooting the same number of minutes the day of the game, eating the same meal, listening to the same music, phoning the same group of people. Others switch themselves on only an hour or so before tipoff, able quickly to concentrate as they tape their ankles, put on their uniform, and do some stretching exercises.

Part of the purpose of the concentration is to get your mind to push your body to its highest possible performance. Bill Russell used to work himself up so much that he would vomit before nearly every game. For high school and college players, there is no excuse for not being "up for the game." They play a limited number of times a year, and the years of competition are finite. In the pros, where you can play over a hundred contests a year, it's more difficult to be up for each one of them. Injuries intervene, fatigue deadens anticipation, opponent quality varies. The essential requirement for victory is that there always be a teammate to pick up the slack. On great teams, someone always steps up. That way, the team continues to win. When you lose because you haven't made the mental effort, you have no one to blame but yourself.

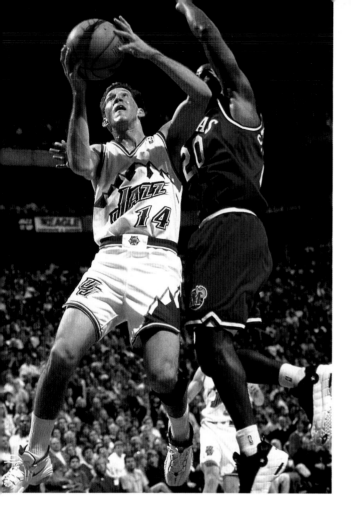

ROLE PLAYING

Jeff Hornacek, Bob Gross, Satch Sanders

Accepting the role that's handed to you can be difficult. Some players can't make the necessary switch from being a scorer to being a passer. But no team can win unless the role players do their jobs. At Utah, the contributions of Jeff Hornacek (left) have helped turn the Jazz into a championship contender. Portland's lone NBA title in 1977 owed much to the talents of its role players, including Bob Gross (right), who set far more screens than he took shots. The Celtics of the 1960s had the wonderful Satch Sanders (opposite page), who created the model of a great role player essential to a team's success.

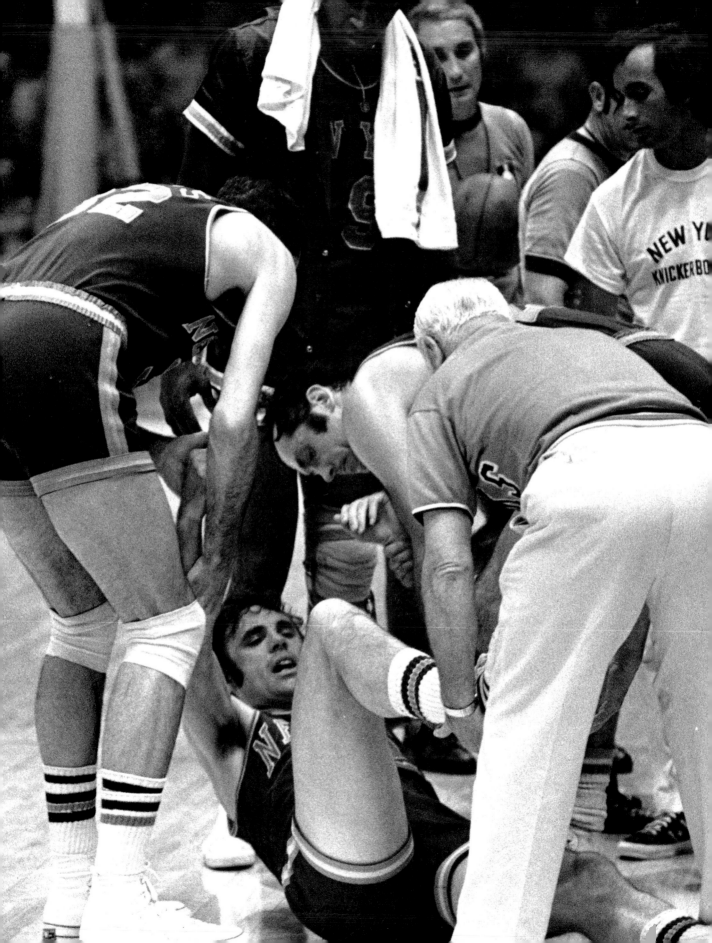

RESILIENCE

BASKETBALL IS A LABORATORY for learning how to handle adversity, which comes in many forms—obvious ones, like injury or defeat, and less tangible ones, like the crowd's contempt or the lengthening of an opponent's lead. Adversity offers a richness of experience all its own, and even victory has pitfalls. Rudyard Kipling told us to "meet with triumph and disaster and treat those two impostors just the same." Unfortunately most of us can't do that. We allow defeat to crush us, or we exult unrealistically in victory.

For me, learning to cope with defeat was not easy. From the time I was in high school, I used to turn a basketball loss over and over in my mind, asking myself what I and others could have done differently. Often I replayed the game so relentlessly that it would interfere with my sleep. The loss hung for days, like a fog: Other people offered analyses, the coach had his interpretations and injunctions, but it took days of practice and the prospect of another game to get a defeat fully behind me.

That pattern continued until my second year in the NBA. I had just made the Knicks starting team as a forward, and we had lost a close one in Philadelphia on a bad pass I made when the Sixers were applying a full-court press. After the game, I was dejected. Back at the hotel, Dave DeBusschere, an experienced pro who had joined the team two months earlier and was my new roommate, put me straight: "You can't go through

STEPPING UP
Dave DeBusschere, New York Knicks

Getting back up after an injury or a loss is necessary in the pros, but sometimes there isn't enough time. In the fifth game of the 1973 NBA finals against the Lakers, Dave DeBusschere severely sprained his ankle. Two more games without him was a risky prospect, so a few of us, led by Earl Monroe, elevated our individual efforts, and we won the championship that night.

a season like this. There are too many games. Sure, you blew it tonight, but when it's over, it's over. Let it go. Otherwise you won't be ready to play tomorrow night." That piece of advice helped change my whole attitude. Even a good pro team is going to lose twenty games a year. I realized that the more you carry the bad past around with you in the present, the less likely it is that the future will improve.

Victory is the more subtle impostor. When you begin to expect it as a continuum instead of seeing it as a reward that has to be fought for, you're in trouble. Julius Erving once said that sustaining focus after a failure isn't a problem—indeed, it might even sharpen your alertness because you'd be intent on making up for the mistake. It's after you've pulled off a great play that focus is difficult, because there's "a strong temptation to dwell on what you just did." By the time you finish congratulating yourself, your opponent has scored three baskets.

The ultimate danger of being victorious is losing sight of how you got there. Only a few teams in the NBA have repeated as champions. As Bill Russell puts it: "It's easier to become Number One than it is to stay Number One." Somewhere along the line, most teams fail to prepare themselves for the season following a championship. The fault can be mental, as in the lessening of the desire to win, or physical, as in reporting to training camp overweight or undertrained. Occasionally jealousy among players about who got what rewards out of the last year's championship can eat away at team unity.

Bouncing back from both victory and defeat requires a reservoir of self-knowledge. Making adjustments in your playing style is sometimes wise, but altering what you believe about the game in order to break a skid will never work. Nearly every day Phil Jackson puts on the chalkboard a clearly defined set of offensive principles: Provide proper spacing, penetrate the defense, ensure player and ball movement

REBOUND
Chicago Bulls, 1997

As any defending champion knows, staying on top takes an extra measure of resolve. Everyone wants to knock off the champ. One reason the Bulls have been able to extend their reign is the partnership of Michael Jordan and his running mate, Scottie Pippen. They have continually challenged each other and their teammates to achieve a higher level of excellence.

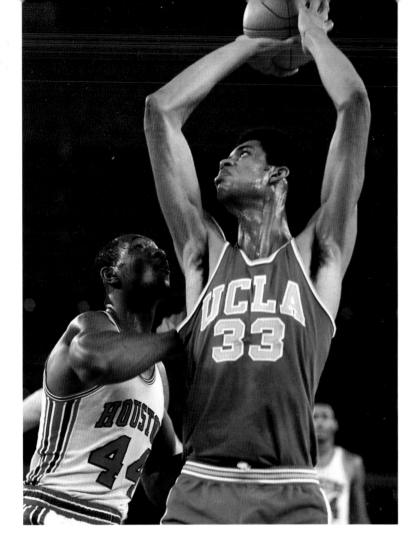

COPING WITH LOSS
Lew Alcindor (Kareem Abdul-Jabbar)

It was one of the biggest showcase games ever played in college basketball: Lew Alcindor's UCLA Bruins against Elvin Hayes's Houston Cougars before 55,000 people in the Houston Astrodome, January 1968. Things didn't go well for UCLA or Alcindor, who had been suffering from a serious eye injury. He was determined to make amends for the loss if he ever got the chance. He did, when UCLA beat Houston badly in the NCAA tournament the same season.

with a purpose, provide strong rebounding position and good defensive balance on all shots, and so on. A set of principles allows a coach's criticism to be less personal and each player's performance to be measured against the team mission. If your game is guided that way, it's easier to be consistent. Otherwise, you're just reacting—to helpful friends or critical sportswriters, all with their own ideas about how you won or what went wrong. While it's a good idea to take praise in the press with a grain of salt, it's also wise to listen to the criticisim and determine whether or not it's merited. If it's not, treat it just like the praise.

There's also a need for such a thing as resilience within a game. In most contests, there are good and bad moments; the flow is inevitable. Yet some players, and some teams, can't seem to come back from a bad break. When a team makes a few dumb plays or gets a few bad calls, its play often deteriorates. Teammates will glare at each other; occasionally, hostile words will pass between them. By the fourth quarter, they're starting to prepare their postgame excuses. Defeat is inevitable. When things go bad for such teams, no one steps in to change the momentum, and then they get even worse.

There is no greater tonic for team morale than a come-from-behind victory; it's the core of team resilience. In 1972, the Knicks fell 19 points behind Milwaukee in a game with six minutes to go, yet we won. When our team hit a few shots while holding the Bucks scoreless, the crowd in Madison Square Garden began to rumble. After a few steals were converted into baskets, the margin dropped to 8 points, and the rumble turned into a roar. By the time we trailed by only 2 points, the roar was deafening. By the end of the game, which we won, people were shouting, "I believe! I believe!" convinced that we could overcome any obstacle, surmount any lead.

That belief has remarkable power. Combined with trust in your teammates, it can have a dramatic psychological effect on your opponents. It becomes a part of your team's reputation. Once that happens, no opposing team ever feels safe, no matter how great a lead it has. More important, your team knows it will be in every game until the very end.

COMEBACK STORIES, examples of tenacity under pressure, provide a model for beating the odds. They become part of the collective imagination, and they are drawn on in countless situations by people in all walks of life. The stories tell us never to give up—that failure can turn to success, that misfortune can be overcome, that the human spirit is indomitable, and that all of us are stronger working with one another than we are working alone.

In basketball, there is no misfortune greater than injury. A player's career can end with one twist of the knee or ankle. In few other activities is such finality so closely wedded to such physical virtuosity. While most injuries are temporary, the healing process isn't complete until the player returns to the game. When you are injured, your first thought is "How soon can I play again?"—followed by fear that the answer is "Never."

The very thought that injury can end a career focuses your energy in a peculiar way. When you're recuperating, life looks different. It did for me in 1961, in the summer after my senior year in high school. I had broken my foot in a baseball game, and as I sat with it in a cast I contemplated a world without basketball. Where would I go to college if there was to be no more basketball? A few weeks after I posed that question to myself, I decided not to go to Duke, where I had accepted an athletic scholarship, but to enroll instead at Princeton, where I had none. If I hadn't injured my foot, I might never have made the switch.

Amy Cook is the daughter of a friend of mine. Her father was a high school track coach, whose teams had won six state championships. His greatest satisfaction, however, came from seeing his daughter grow up to be a great 100-meter high hurdler. In her sophomore year in high school, she had the fastest recorded time in the state of Missouri and won second place in the state championship. Then, in the winter of her junior year, she tore her anterior cruciate ligament during the district basketball finals. She had surgery and reconstruction of the knee joint. The doctors said that it was uncertain if she would ever run again. The cast stayed on for eight weeks and then she began the rehabilitation—the weight clinic, the stretches, the jogging— hoping to get ready for her senior year season. Her parents accompanied her every morning to her 6:30 workouts. She returned to competition in March of her senior year, but she didn't do well. Sometimes she couldn't even finish a race because of the pain. She barely qualified for the state championships—and as she and her father drove to Jefferson City for the state meet, they knew they had both done everything they possibly could to prepare her for the event. When the runners took their mark, Amy's father was close to tears, afraid that his daughter would be crushed by a poor performance. The gun went off and Amy jumped out ahead, holding the lead to the finish.

Amy Cook was the state champion. She had reached deep into herself and found the confidence and drive that enabled her to win. It was partly physical—she had done everything she could to get ready. It was partly mental—she had prepared herself to risk everything in order to win. But it was her resilience that put her over the top.

A PART OF BEING resilient is understanding that there are some things in life that can never be gotten over, no matter how many games are under your belt. I felt sad on many levels on November 7, 1991, when Magic Johnson reported to the world that he was infected with HIV. I mourned the loss to the game. Yet Magic's terrible misfortune reminds us that each of us harbors self-destructive impulses and urges, along with all the qualities we're proudest of. By standing up in public and telling young people, "Don't make the mistakes I made," Magic shed some light on a part of our human nature that is too often hidden. For that gift from him, we must be grateful.

It may be that by accepting the limits to resilience we can celebrate it, using it when we can and cherishing it while it lasts. I've made it through more than a few tough moments in my life by drawing on the resources of my basketball years. Resilience is what allows us to struggle hard and long with tragedy or loss or misfortune or change and still manage to dig deep and find our second wind. It is a kind of toughness. Each life blow no longer shatters us like a hammer hitting brick; rather, it makes us stronger. It tempers us, like a hammer hitting metal. Imagine the comfort in knowing that by never giving up, by accepting the bad breaks and going on, you will have lived life to the fullest, and maybe will have lived it a little longer. Such peace of mind is often reward enough.

DEFEAT

Losing can be harsh, unfair—particularly in the NCAA tournament, where one loss means a crushing end to your season. For college players, the emotion of a loss can be devastating. But even the best NBA teams can count on losing fifteen to twenty-five games a season, and more in the playoffs. You don't have to like defeat, but you've got to accept it. In the early part of my career, losing tore me up, until I learned to learn from it, deal with it, and move on to the next game.

IMAGINATION

THE INNOVATORS IN BASKETBALL came upon their ideas through trial and error, by playing the game. Hank Luisetti of Stanford was the first player to shoot with one hand; before that, all basketball shots except the layup and the hook were two-handed. Joe Fulks of the Philadelphia Warriors concluded that he could get the edge on his opponent if he jumped and shot the ball from the top of his leap, and the jump shot was born. In the 1950s, Bob Cousy began passing the ball behind his back. He was considered a hot dog by traditionalists, but like most innovators he persisted because he believed in his idea—besides, the crowds loved it. Gradually, coaches saw that the efficiency and deceptiveness of the move paid off in easier baskets for teammates. About that time, Elgin Baylor entered the pro ranks. Baylor's tremendous leaping ability allowed him to combine the jump shot and layup; he was the first player who seemed to hang in air, defying gravity. Julius Erving and Michael Jordan are his direct descendants. Even kids with no leaping ability (myself included—the joke on the Knicks was that my peak leap equaled the thickness of a Sunday *New York Times*) tried to imitate Elgin as he moved around the basket, altering his shot by changing the ball from hand to hand and using the rim on layups to block his defender's attempt to reach the ball.

Innovation took place mainly on offense until Bill Russell and K. C. Jones arrived on the scene in the mid-fifties. As teammates on consecutive national

HANK LUISETTI
Stanford, 1938

He never played in the NBA, but Stanford's Hank Luisetti had a profound effect on the game. He had the courage to defy the conventional wisdom of the 1930s and start taking his shots with one hand. It was a counterintuitive notion—wouldn't you get more control using two hands?—but Luisetti, sensing that with one hand he had a quicker release and greater flexibility, promptly proved otherwise.

championship teams at the University of San Francisco, and then on the Celtics championship teams, they changed the meaning of defense in basketball. Before them, it was like counterpunching in boxing: The offense would make a move and the defense would respond to it. Russell and Jones forced the offense to react. "K. C. thought differently," Russell wrote in his book, *Second Wind:*

"He was always figuring ways he could make the opponent take the shot he wanted him to take when he wanted him to take it, from the place he wanted the man to shoot. Often during games, he would pretend to stumble into my man while letting the player he was guarding have a free drive to the basket with the ball, knowing that I could block the shot and take the ball away. Or, he'd let a man have an outside shot from just beyond the perimeter of his effectiveness and, instead of harassing the player, would take off down the court, figuring that I'd get the rebound and throw him a long pass for an easy basket."

Russell in particular was a master of invention. Having concluded that horizontal lines defined the game better than vertical ones (notwithstanding the fact that more and more players were jumping higher), he was always conscious of the angle at which he did anything on the court. If he had to block a shot from behind on a man streaking for a breakaway layup, he would take a step to the left so that he could come from behind at an angle that would allow his left arm to block the shot and his body to land to the shooter's right, thereby avoiding the collision that would have earned him a foul. If he was attempting to block a jump shot, he tried to do it during the first foot of the ball's arc, which meant that his body had to be close to the shooter's body in the air; and he used a vertical leap with outstretched arms because that created fewer fouls than a leap forward, which would have carried his body into the shooter. He also knew that while a

ONE-MAN DEFENSIVE PLAN
Bill Russell

"In addition to being physically gifted, he was always the smartest guy out on the floor," John Havlicek said of Bill Russell, the Celtics center. Russell's almost scientific approach to defense changed the way the game is played, and his shot-blocking ability forced many teams to alter their offense. More than a few players missed open layups because they heard his footsteps.

blocked shot pleases the crowd, it is only half the story; the other half is giving your team control of the ball. So when he blocked a shot, his aim was to bat the ball not into the crowd or against the backboard but to a teammate so that the fast break could begin.

Russell also pointed out that over 60 percent of rebounds occur below the rim, which means that positioning is more important than leaping ability. Knowing where a particular player's shot usually bounces allows you to anticipate where to be. Boxing out far enough from the basket increases the area you can reach whenever the ball caroms off the rim. Starting under the basket and backing (or assing) your opponent out toward the foul line can surprise him and create a similar space to gather in a rebound. More than any other player then or

REBOUNDING
Location, Location, Location

Underneath the boards is the no-man's-land of basketball, a place where bodies smash into each other and where all sorts of mayhem takes place in the fight for rebounds. The Nets' Jayson Williams (left) is a great positional rebounder. Paul Silas of the Sonics (right) demonstrates another method of moving your man out of the way.

since, Russell mastered the game's mental aspects, but other great rebounders—Paul Silas, Dave DeBusschere, Moses Malone, Dennis Rodman, Jayson Williams—also understand the subtlety of the art.

The most dramatic sports innovation I can recall was introduced by the high jumper Dick Fosbury in 1968, when he turned on his back going over the bar instead of going over stomach down, which was the conventional approach. "I was told over and over again that I would never be successful, that I was not going to be competitive and the technique was simply not going to work," he said to a reporter after winning the gold medal at the Mexico City Olympics. "All I could do was shrug and say, 'We'll just have to see.'" The artist, the scientist in the lab, the technologist with a hunch develop ideas that change the world forever. These sports innovators remind us anew that one person can make a difference—and has, time and time again.

Some players demonstrate a creative imagination in maximizing their modest skills. One of my teammates once said to me half jokingly, "You know, Bill, you're the best player in the NBA—from your wrist to the tip of your fingers." He meant that I had good hands, hands that got to a lot of places quickly. Often you can block an opponent's shot by sticking your hand into the area where he brings the ball up from a dribble for the shot, a move called "stripping him." When the Knicks played a team with a big center, I would often drop off my man and double team the center when he got the ball. More than a few times, while I was still facing the man I was guarding, I would reach back with my swatting hand and knock the ball loose from the center's grip. At a minimum I clogged up the area so that the center had less room to make his move.

Having good hands on offense means that you can catch a pass, make a pass, catch and flick a pass at will. In shooting, good hands help to produce a quick release—the speed with which you move the ball from where you received it to shooting position. Beyond good hands, really great passers have a kind of sixth sense that is spatial and rooted in superb eye-hand coordination and unusual peripheral and depth vision. And really great shooters plant their feet so that they have balance when they

The ability to improve—to see the pass that no one else can see and deliver it, sometimes without looking—has been the hallmark of the game's great guards. Magic Johnson (32, opposite page) could find himself one on three and still confuse the defense as to what he would actually do. (Right) Walt Frazier (10) and Earl Monroe (15) had flare to spare.

receive the ball. Imagination flows into your game when you devise your own ways of combining quick hands, good eyes, and good feet.

SOMETIMES RULE CHANGES force innovations in the way the game is played. The 3-point rule is an example. By giving an extra point for a successful shot 23 feet 9 inches or more from the basket, the rule turned the game upside down. Before the 1979–80 season, the objective was to get the easiest shot, as close as possible to the basket. There was a maximum of player movement, with a premium on finesse and team coordination. Now you're more likely to see a screen-and-roll on one side of the floor, with six players standing far from the basket on the opposite side of the floor. If you don't get a clear jump shot or a layup off the screen-and-roll, you drive with the ball. If you get nowhere because of a double team, you simply kick it out to a teammate waiting for the ball behind the 3-point line. Too often, strategies are devised to get an open twenty-five-foot shot as much as to get a layup.

The 3-point rule created a whole new market for good spot shooters—players of average overall skills who could hit the open, standing twenty-five-footer with great regularity: Dell Curry of Charlotte, Steve Kerr of the Chicago Bulls, and Dale Ellis of the Seattle SuperSonics are examples. Since many of my shots as a pro were near that range, people have asked me if I wish I had played when the rule was in effect. My answer is no. What you give up in team movement and finesse is not worth what you get from a few extra points beyond the 3-point line.

IMAGINATION CAN ALSO stretch the rules, for basketball is a game of subtle felonies. Referees have a wide latitude in determining whether or not an infraction has taken place. Sometimes they will ignore the rules. For example, you have to dribble the ball with your hand on top or on the side of the ball; if you put your hand under the ball to initiate or continue the dribble, you should be charged with palming or carrying the ball. Now, increasingly in the pros, referees don't call it. They allow players to palm the ball, particularly on the crossover dribble. That change has allowed players with great quickness, such as Stephon Marbury of the Minnesota Timberwolves and Allen Iverson of the Philadelphia 76ers, to use the crossover move with great effectiveness.

Players can use their creativity to shape the referee's interpretation or even to avoid his detection. I can remember the excitement I felt when I was exposed to this game within the game. Jerry West told me how to hook my left hand around an opponent's leg to get leverage when I whirled around him. Ed Macauley showed me how to place my foot to the side of my man before I received a pass, so that when I got the ball I would have already beaten him by half a step. Macauley also showed me how to maintain awareness of where my man was on defense when I wasn't looking at him directly: keeping my hands in constant touch with him as if I were reading Braille. I learned by watching Cliff Hagan and Elgin Baylor how to fend off an opponent's attempt to block your shot by using your free hand to protect the ball from his reach.

The writer Frank Deford once noted in an article on Boston Celtics swing man Frank Ramsey that about 20 percent of a team's points in the average game come from free throws. The more you can sucker your opponent into committing fouls, the more points you can add to your team total. Ramsey was full of tricks. He could draw an offensive foul by placing his hand behind his opponent's back (the hand away from the referee) and pulling him forward so that it would appear that the opponent had intentionally run into him. On defensive rebounds, if his opponent had nudged him under the basket so that he couldn't get to the ball, he would simply fling up his arms and fall forward, looking for all the world like a man who had been pushed. Often the referee agreed. He also perfected the art of getting an opponent to jump to block an anticipated shot and

BEYOND THE ARC

The 3-point shot is not just another way to score; it has changed the way basketball is played, and not necessarily for the better. The 3-point line has also created unique job opportunities for long-range bombers such as Chicago's Steve Kerr (left) and Seattle's Dale Ellis (right).

then leaning into him while he's suspended helpless in the air so that he grazes you on his way down and your way up for the shot. That way he doesn't disturb your shot and the referee is likely to call a foul on him. (This was a technique I used to great advantage throughout my college years; in the pros, fewer calls came my way, so I abandoned it.) You see moves like this every day in the college and NBA season—they involve creative deception and challenge the referee's skills as aggressively as those of the opponent. (Michael Jordan's heroic last-second shot in the 1998 NBA finals was aided by the clever use of his left hand to nudge Bryon Russell off balance just before Jordan pulled up and hit the shot.)

TALKING A GOOD GAME
Reggie Miller, Gary Payton, Larry Bird

Talk is no longer cheap in the NBA, not with today's salaries; the wrong words in public can cost you in league fines. But talk does have its place. (Left to right) The Pacers' Reggie Miller can chatter away while drilling shot after shot. Seattle's Gary Payton will wear down an opponent verbally and mentally—even a fellow speechmaker like Charles Barkley. Larry Bird was notorious for aggravating his opponent to distraction.

Much attention has focused on trash talk in recent years, particularly its ugly and hostile varieties, but using talk to disturb your opponent's concentration has been around a long time. As a high school player, I used to play a foul-shooting game in which it was permissible to do anything to the shooter except touch him or obstruct his vision. The purpose of shouting at him, making jokes at his expense, and insulting him was to get him to break his concentration, and it was good preparation for the pressures of the game itself. The distinction worth drawing is between flagrant talk for show, which the crowd sees, and subtle talk for results, which it doesn't see. Talk for results takes many forms, but it usually means trying to rattle your opponent. It could be Sam Jones of the Celtics saying to Wilt Chamberlain, after Wilt failed to block a shot, "Too late, baby!" Or it could be Bill Russell looking at me during a foul shot and then at Satch Sanders, who was guarding me, and saying exasperatedly, "Come on, Satch, don't let *him* score!" It could be Michael Jordan saying to a rookie on the opposing team before closing his eyes and making the free throw, "Hey, rook, I bet you can't do this." It could be Larry Bird telling his opponent before the game, in the hallway leading to the court, "I think I'm really feeling good tonight. I think I might go for about fifty." Or Bird, when Michael Jordan in his early years guarded him on a switch, saying, "I got a little one—give me the ball!" Or Bird during one holiday game, scoring on his man and then wishing him a Merry Christmas. Sportswriter Peter DeJonge has written, "What made Bird untouchable was the seamless connection between his dribbling and babbling, as if his tongue were one more incredibly coordinated limb. As he backed his defender down, Bird would matter-of-factly tell him where they were going and what was going to happen when they got there, going on to explain that his being able to do exactly what he wanted, and the defender being helpless to do anything but watch, was the reason for the huge discrepancy in their salaries. In the middle of this combination radio play-by-play and TV color commentary, without any telltale grunt, the ball would be flying toward the basket with the concluding remarks: 'Don't even turn around. It's all net.'"

JERRY LUCAS WAS ANOTHER player who understood this aspect of the game. When an opponent shot a free throw, we sometimes signaled a play that called for me to fake a move to the far side of the court and instead receive a pass and take an easy jumper behind a Lucas screen. As I began my move to the other side, Jerry would shout angrily, "Get out of here, Bill! Get the hell to the other side! Go!" My man, hearing this, would retreat a couple of steps in anticipation of my move across court, and then I would quickly step behind the screen for an uncontested shot. Or during a game Jerry and I would converse in gibberish, pretending that we understood each other. "Eee yah see motch eee kah!" I would yell. "Puto rass dee yah!" Lucas would reply. The bewildered defender often would retreat a step, his concentration broken as he tried to anticipate more alternatives than were possible. (What were they saying? It must mean something!) While he was thinking, the ball would go through the basket.

SOMETIMES IT'S IMAGINATION that motivates you in the first place. It enables you to dream. At one time or another, every kid who picks up a basketball pictures himself or herself a court star.

The basket in my backyard was put up when I was ten years old. A year later, the wooden poles were replaced by a steel pole and a metal fan-shaped backboard. My parents also laid down a twelve-by-sixteen-foot strip of asphalt and put spotlights on the garage so I could practice after it got dark. I felt like a king, presiding over the Cadillac of backyard courts in our small town. When I was in the fifth and sixth grades, you could find me out there every day after school shooting until dinner. In the winter, I'd wear gloves and a wool hat and two sweatshirts. Occasionally neighborhood kids would join me in a game of H-O-R-S-E. After a while there'd be enough of us to play a half-court game. Because I was taller than the others, we made it a condition of play that I couldn't shoot any closer than ten feet from the basket. Backyard one-on-one games were where the juices of competition first rose within me. Pride prevented me from calling a foul against my opponent when he pushed me or hacked my arm. Contact led to more contact, but it stopped short of an exchange of blows. Controlling my temper in such circumstances was just one of the lessons I learned in the backyard.

Sometimes my mother would come outdoors to challenge me. Not too long ago, I was looking through an old photo album and came across a picture of her, dark-eyed and beautiful, with her shining brown hair pulled back from her face, sitting with her teammates on the 1927 Herculaneum High School basketball team, of which she and her best friend, "Nooks" Dugan, were the unquestioned stars. Twenty years after her high school triumphs, she still considered herself a player, and she still wanted to win when we played one on one. Once when I was in the seventh grade, she gave me a little push going for the steal, and I pushed her back—whereupon, to my horror, she slipped and cracked her skull on the asphalt. I was petrified, but she got up, just smiled, and called it quits—at least for that day.

I remember the Saturday afternoon in 1958 when the St. Louis Hawks beat the Boston Celtics for the NBA championship. In my mind, I was one of them. I was Bob Pettit shooting the standing jumper, or Cliff Hagan mixing his sweeping hook with reverse layups. Shortly after the game, I went out to the backyard for practice and imagined myself hitting the winning shot. "Four seconds left, three, two—Bradley shoots . . . it's good!"

Nothing unique about that. Thousands of kids all over America, on a winter afternoon at the playground, or out behind the barn, or on the driveway, imagine that they will someday score the winning basket, maybe even in the pros. They sense they may be a step too slow, but then who knows for sure? "It's dropping today. . . . Only nets. . . . Time after time. . . . One more against the board." *Bong! Swish!* Jumper left . . . *swish!* Jumper right . . . *swish!* Left hook . . . *swish!* "Feel the ball in your hands. . . . Who does know for sure? . . . Just keep practicing. . . . Just keep shooting. . . . Maybe next year, I'll be a little taller. . . ."

DREAM MAKERS
St. Louis Hawks, 1958

We need real-life inspiration for our
basketball dreams. While I was
growing up in Missouri, mine was
the St. Louis Hawks, led by my
first basketball hero, Bob Pettit (9),
who hit for 50 to clinch the 1958
championship with the help of Easy
Ed Macauley and Cliff Hagan.

Inevitably, in those moments of solitary practice, you imagined the voice of
your favorite team's broadcaster. Buddy Blattner covered the St. Louis Hawks, painting
vivid word pictures of the game and its players—George "the Bird" Yardley of the Fort
Wayne Pistons, Maurice Stokes of Rochester, Sweetwater Clifton of the Knicks, Wilt
the Stilt of Philadelphia. Sitting at my desk in my bedroom, I would tune in between,
and occasionally during, my various homework assignments. (I sometimes wonder
what effect that nonstop crackling play-by-play had on my Latin.) The most famous
radio sportscaster of all was Marty Glickman of the New York Knicks, who was also the
announcer on the annual Converse All-Star highlights film. More than a few young
boys in the fifties fell asleep listening to the transistor under the pillow, lullabied, as
the poet Bob Mitchell says, "by the mellifluent tones of the great Marty Glickmanese":

BILL BRADLEY

Now it's Braun passing to Dick McGuire,

Now back to Carl at the top of the key for a two-hand pop:

Gooooood! Like Nedick's!

Yes!

Now it's Dolph Schayes getting a pass from Seymour,

He slices to his right, he drives past Gallatin,

He lays it up, it's good and he's fouled!

IMAGINATION LOOKS FORWARD when you're a ten-year-old shooting in the driveway. When you reach an age at which you can no longer play competitively, you start looking back. Basketball, unlike golf or tennis, is only for the young. Unless you don't mind popping an Achilles tendon, you should retire from the game by age forty. A few old high school stars go longer, but most play only in their memories. Life's other tasks take over, and for some, like Rabbit Angstrom in John Updike's *Rabbit, Run,* there is nothing else in life that has ever quite matched the feeling you had when you were playing the game before the crowd, when you were young and a star. And then you arrive at an age when you relish life in a new and different way. The sense of lost youth is gone—the challenge now is to make the most of the time left to you—and you can more deeply appreciate the role the game has played in your life. It has become more than just memories; it has become almost an essential part of you.

Imagination allows us to escape the predictable. Artists, scientists, poets use the power of imagination every day. For those of us who found it in playing the game, it has shaped our joy in countless ways. It has enriched our experience and allowed us to feel the thrill of fresh creation. It puts us in touch with what most makes us human. Above all, it enables us to see beyond the moment, to transcend our circumstances however dire they appear, and to reply to the common wisdom that says we cannot soar by saying, "Just watch!"

NOT-SO-SUBTLE FELONIES

Willis Reed and Dave Cowens, Allen Iverson, Tracy Reid

All rules are open to interpretation, and Willis Reed (19) and Dave Cowens (opposite page) demonstrate the gray area that exists in the paint under the basket.
Sometimes innovators force the rule makers to look the other way. Philadelphia's
Allen Iverson (left) leaves defenders behind with the league's fastest crossover
dribble, which once upon a time was called a carry. But you've got to make space
where you can, an art not lost on North Carolina's Tracy Reid, either (right).

INNOVATIONS

George Gervin, Earl Monroe, Julius Erving

Basketball is a team game that has always relied on individual creativity to make it more exciting. George "The Iceman" Gervin (left) gave us the forward finger roll, a devious last flip that drove would-be blockers to distraction. Earl "The Pearl" Monroe (right) had a repertory of moves (head faking, shoulder faking, spinning, stutter stepping, double pumping) that made him one of the most elusive guards in the game and a fan favorite. Dr. J (opposite page) took what Elgin Baylor had done and squared it. He not only defied gravity but was a player of such prodigious talent that he could make up his mind what to do while he was in the air, then do it. And all of his fans soared with him.

Page 1, Damian Strohmeyer/*Sports Illustrated*; page 2, George Kalinsky; pages 4–5, Lane Stewart/*Sports Illustrated*; page 6, Anthony Neste/*Sports Illustrated*; page 8, Rayrose (left), Bruce Roberts/*Sports Illustrated* (center), Associated Press (right); page 12, George Kalinsky; page 14, *St. Louis Post-Dispatch* (left), Bruce Roberts/*Sports Illustrated* (right); page 15, Roy DeCarava/*Sports Illustrated* (left), Walter Iooss Jr./*Sports Illustrated* (right); page 16, Joe McNally/*Sports Illustrated*; page 19, Herb Scharfman/*Sports Illustrated*; page 20, David E. Klutho/*Sports Illustrated*; page 22, George Kalinsky; page 24, Barry Gossage/NBA Photos; page 25, Doug Pensiger/Allsport (left), John W. McDonough/*Sports Illustrated* (right); page 26, Bill Baptist/NBA Photos (left), Rick Stewart/Allsport (right); page 27, Jennifer Potheiser/NBA Photos; page 28, Walter Iooss Jr./*Sports Illustrated*; page 30, George Kalinsky; page 32, George Kalinsky; page 33, Peter Read Miller/*Sports Illustrated* (left), Gerry Cranham/*Sports Illustrated* (right); page 35, Steve Lipofsky; page 37, Richard Mackson/*Sports Illustrated*; page 38, Tim O'Dell/NBA Photos (left), Dick Raphael/NBA Photos (right); page 39, Walter Iooss Jr./*Sports Illustrated*; page 40, Walter Iooss Jr./*Sports Illustrated*; page 41, Brian Bahr/Allsport (left), Tim DeFrisco/NBA Photos (right); page 42, Tim DeFrisco; page 45, George Kalinsky; page 46, Walter Iooss Jr./*Sports Illustrated*; pages 48–49, John W. McDonough/*Sports Illustrated*; page 51, Walter Iooss Jr./*Sports Illustrated*; page 53, Steve Lipofsky; page 54, George Kalinsky; page 55, Manny Millan/*Sports Illustrated* (left), Richard Mackson/*Sports Illustrated* (right); page 56, Norm Perdue/NBA Photos (left), Heinz Kluetmeier/*Sports Illustrated* (right); page 57, Jerry Cabluck/*Sports Illustrated*; page 58, Walter Iooss Jr./*Sports Illustrated*; page 61; Bruce L. Schwartzman; page 62, Sheedy & Long/*Sports Illustrated* (left), Peter Read Miller/*Sports Illustrated* (right); page 65, Louis Psihoyos/*Sports Illustrated*; page 66, Patrick Murphy-Racey/*Sports Illustrated*; page 68, Victor Baldizon/NBA Photos; page 69, Bill Baptist/NBA Photos; page 70, John W. McDonough/*Sports Illustrated*; page 71, John W. McDonough; page 72, David Liam Kyle/NBA Photos; page 73, Jonathan Daniel/Allsport; page 74, Bruce Roberts/*Sports Illustrated*; page 77, Rich Clarkson/*Sports Illustrated*; page 78, Walter Iooss Jr./*Sports Illustrated*; page 80, UPI/Corbis-Bettmann; page 81, George Kalinsky; page 82, George Kalinsky; pages 84–85, Walter Iooss Jr./*Sports Illustrated*; page 86, Jonathan Daniel/Allsport; page 89, Associated Press; page 90, Lou Capozzola/NBA Photos; page 93, George Kalinsky; page 94, Andrew D. Bernstein/NBA Photos; pages 96–97, Nathaniel S. Butler/NBA Photos; page 98, Sam Forencich/NBA Photos; page 99, Lou Capozzola/NBA Photos; page 100, George Kalinsky; page 101, John D. Hanlon/*Sports Illustrated* (left and center), Sheedy & Long/*Sports Illustrated* (right); page 102, Naismith Memorial Basketball Hall of Fame; page 104, Manny Millan/*Sports Illustrated*; page 105, Chuck Solomon/*Sports Illustrated*; page 107, Andy Hayt/NBA Photos (left), Walter Iooss Jr./*Sports Illustrated* (center), Patrick Murphy-Racey/*Sports Illustrated* (right); page 108, Bruce L. Schwartzman; page 111, Naismith Memorial Basketball Hall of Fame; page 112, John W. McDonough/*Sports Illustrated*; page 114, James Drake/*Sports Illustrated*; page 115, Peter Read Miller/*Sports Illustrated* (left), Bill Baptist/NBA Photos (center), Nathaniel S. Butler/NBA Photos (right); page 116, Rich Clarkson/*Sports Illustrated*; page 117, Bruce L. Schwartzman (left), Nathaniel S. Butler/NBA Photos (right); page 118, Fernando Medina/Allsport; page 120, George Kalinsky; page 123, Allsport; page 124, George Kalinsky; page 126, Associated Press; page 127, Associated Press; page 128, Norm Perdue/NBA Photos (left), Hank Delespinasse/*Sports Illustrated* (right); page 129, Walter Iooss Jr./*Sports Illustrated*; page 130, George Kalinsky; page 133, John W. McDonough/*Sports Illustrated*; page 134, Neil Leifer/*Sports Illustrated*; page 138, Dick Raphael/NBA Photos; page 139, Jonathan Daniel/Allsport (left), Carl Skalak/NBA Photos (right); page 140, Associated Press; page 143, Sheedy & Long/*Sports Illustrated*; page 144, Noren Trotman/NBA Photos (left), Scott Cunningham/NBA Photos (right); page 146, John W. McDonough/*Sports Illustrated*; page 147, George Kalinsky; page 149, Steve Woltmann/NBA Photos (left), Jeff Reinking/NBA Photos (right); page 150, Andy Hayt/NBA Photos (left), Sam Forencich/NBA Photos (center), Nathaniel S. Butler/NBA Photos (right); page 154, NBA Photo Library; page 156, George Kalinsky; page 157, Lou Capozzola/NBA Photos (left), Patrick Murphy-Racey/*Sports Illustrated* (right); page 158, NBA Photo Library (left), Sheedy & Long/*Sports Illustrated* (right); page 159, Neil Leifer/NBA Photos.